Better Homes and Gardens®

Beginner's Cook Book

BETTER HOMES AND GARDENS® BOOKS

Editor: Gerald M. Knox
Art Director: Ernest Shelton
Managing Editor: David A. Kirchner

Food and Nutrition Editor: Nancy Byal
Department Head, Cook Books: Sharyl Heiken
Associate Department Heads: Sandra Granseth,
    Rosemary C. Hutchinson, Elizabeth Woolever
Senior Food Editors: Julie Henderson, Julia Malloy,
    Marcia Stanley
Associate Food Editors: Jill Burmeister, Molly Culbertson,
    Linda Foley, Linda Henry, Lynn Hoppe, Maureen Powers,
    Joyce Trollope
Recipe Development Editor: Marion Viall
Test Kitchen Director: Sharon Stilwell
Test Kitchen Home Economists: Jean Brekke, Kay Cargill,
    Marilyn Cornelius, Maryellyn Krantz, Dianna Nolin,
    Marge Steenson

Associate Art Directors: Linda Ford Vermie, Neoma Alt West,
    Randall Yontz
Copy and Production Editors: Marsha Jahns,
    Mary Helen Schiltz, Carl Voss, David A. Walsh
Assistant Art Directors: Harijs Priekulis, Tom Wegner
Senior Graphic Designers: Alisann Dixon, Lynda Haupert,
    Lyne Neymeyer
Graphic Designers: Mike Burns, Mike Eagleton, Deb Miner,
    Stan Sams, D. Greg Thompson, Darla Whipple,
    Paul Zimmerman

Vice President, Editorial Director: Doris Eby
Group Editorial Services Director: Duane L. Gregg

General Manager: Fred Stines
Director of Publishing: Robert B. Nelson
Vice President, Retail Marketing: Jamie Martin
Vice President, Direct Marketing: Arthur Heydendael

BEGINNER'S COOK BOOK

Editor: Marcia Stanley
Copy and Production Editor: Marsha Jahns
Graphic Designer: Harry Priekulis
Electronic Text Processor: Donna Russell

On the cover: Chili (see recipe, page 13)

Our seal assures you that every recipe in the *Beginner's Cook Book* has been tested in the Better Homes and Gardens® Test Kitchen. This means that each recipe is practical and reliable, and meets our high standards of taste appeal.

Contents

Getting Started

Cooking has never been as much fun or as easy as it is with Better Homes and Gardens® *Beginner's Cook Book,* a book written for adults. If you are a beginning cook, you'll love the explicit directions and step-by-step photos that lead you through the recipes. And if you have experience cooking, you'll find ideas that will expand your repertoire. You'll also find this book packed with information on menu planning, table setting, kitchen equipment, and cooking terms.

Recipes are written in the easy-to-follow style shown here. At the top you'll find the title, time required, and equipment needed. Ingredients are on the left and instructions are in the center. Look for tips to the right of the recipe or in ruled tip boxes.

Generic Recipe

TIME:
00 minutes preparation
00 minutes cooking

EQUIPMENT
wire whisk   vegetable peeler
rubber spatula   small bowl

The ingredients for
the first step
of the recipe
go here.

● This is the method for the first step of
the recipe. It tells you how to combine
the ingredients.

The ingredients for
the second step
of the recipe
go here.

● This is the method for the second step
of the recipe. It tells you how to combine
the ingredients.
    At the end of the method, there is a
statement telling how many servings the
recipe makes.

If there is any additional
information to go with a
recipe, it appears in either
a recipe sidebar or in a
recipe tip. The sidebar
appears here, next to the
recipe. And if there is a
tip, it will appear in a
ruled box somewhere else
on the page.

1⅓ cups all-purpose
2 tablespoons grat
    Parmesan chee
1 tablespoon snipp
    parsley
easpoon salt
sh garlic powe

lks
e can be
n olive
oil

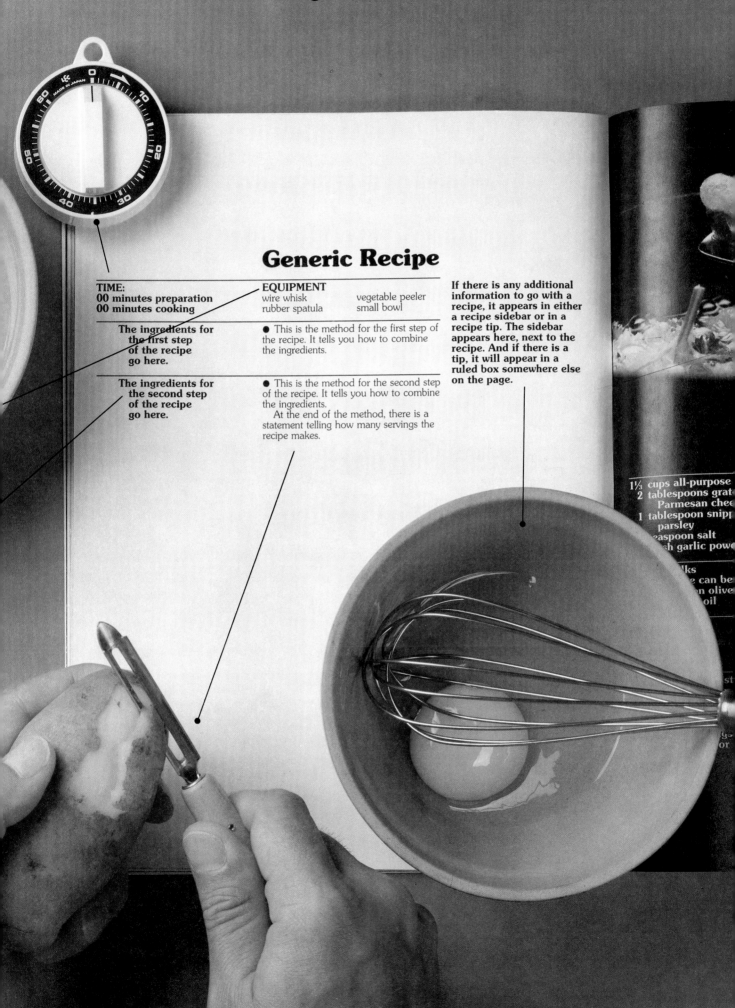

Equipment Basics

Colander

Liquid Measure

Saucepan

Pastry Blender

Rolling Pin

Meat Mallet

CHICAGO CUTLERY 2025

Pancake Turner

Shredder

Fine Shredder

Timer

Serrated Knife

Dutch Oven

Broiler Pan with Rack

Dry Measures

Measuring
Spoons

Wooden
Spoon

Rubber
Spatula

Ladle

Muffin Pan

Baking Sheet
or
Cookie Sheet

Tongs

Chef's
Knife

Boning
Knife

Wire Whisk

Pastry Brush

Cooking Terms

If you're a beginning cook—or even a more experienced cook—sometimes the basic cooking terms and techniques can mystify you. But you don't have to fear cooking terms and techniques you don't know. Just read these tips and you'll become a pro at all kinds of cooking tasks, whether it's measuring milk, measuring flour, shredding cheese, crushing herbs, or finely shredding orange peel.

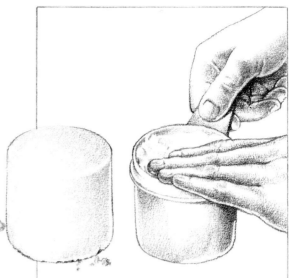

● **Measuring Brown Sugar:** Pack the brown sugar into a dry measure with your hand. Level with a metal spatula. The brown sugar should hold the shape of the measure when it is turned out.

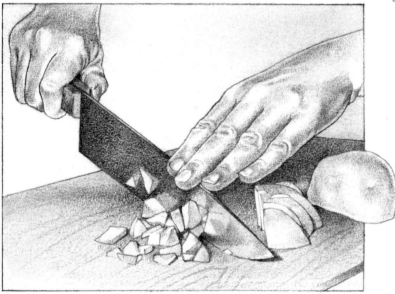

● **Chopping:** Use a chef's knife, blender, or food processor to cut the desired ingredient into small, irregularly shaped pieces about the size of a pea.

● **Beating Eggs:** Holding the egg over a bowl, use a knife to crack the shell in the center. Allow the whole egg to fall into the bowl, and discard the shell. Use a fork to beat the egg till the white and yolk are completely combined with no streaks remaining.

● **Dash:** When a recipe calls for a dash, put in less than $\frac{1}{8}$ teaspoon—about $\frac{1}{16}$ teaspoon.

● **Measuring Shortening:** Use a rubber spatula to pack the shortening into a dry measure. Run a spatula through it to get rid of any air pockets.

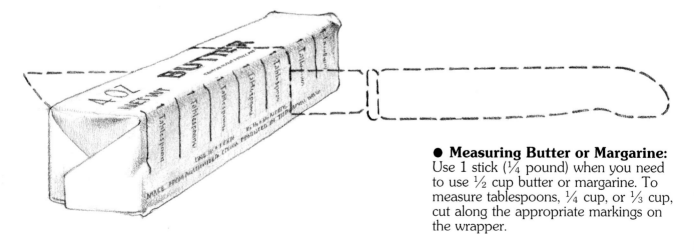

● **Measuring Butter or Margarine:** Use 1 stick ($\frac{1}{4}$ pound) when you need to use $\frac{1}{2}$ cup butter or margarine. To measure tablespoons, $\frac{1}{4}$ cup, or $\frac{1}{3}$ cup, cut along the appropriate markings on the wrapper.

● **Measuring Dried Herbs:** Lightly fill the appropriate measuring spoon to the top, keeping the herb as level as possible with the top. Empty the spoon into your hand and crush the herb with your fingers. This breaks the leaves to better release their flavor.

● **Folding:** Cut down through the mixture with a rubber spatula, scraping across the bottom of the bowl and bringing the spatula up and over the mixture close to the surface. Repeat this down-up-and-over procedure, turning the bowl, until the mixture is combined.

● **Finely Shredding:** Rub the ingredient to be shredded against the smallest holes on your shredder.

● **Measuring Liquids:** Place a liquid measuring cup on a level surface and bend down so that your eyes are level with the marking you wish to read. Fill the cup to the marking.

● **Shredding:** Cut the ingredient into long narrow strips (shred) by rubbing it against the shredder surface that has medium-size or large holes.

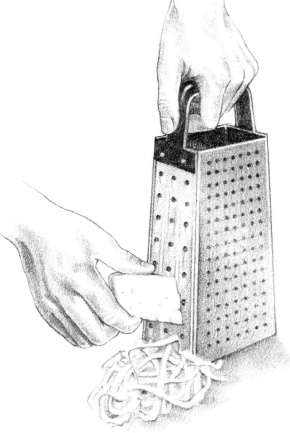

● **Measuring Dry Ingredients:** Use a dry measure with the capacity you wish to measure. Spoon the ingredient into the measure, then level it with a metal spatula. Never pack ingredients, except shortening and brown sugar.

Boiling

Boiling is cooking liquids until they are hot enough to form bubbles that rise in a steady pattern and break on the surface. As the bubbling begins, the whole mass of liquid starts to move. Be sure to notice the difference between boiling and simmering (see below).

Simmering

Simmering is cooking liquids only until they are hot enough for a few bubbles to form slowly and burst below the surface. This is not the same as boiling (see above). Simmering takes place at a lower temperature than boiling, so you'll have to adjust the heat carefully.

Steaming

Steaming is a term for cooking food in the steam given off by boiling water. To steam a food, place it in a perforated metal basket or on a wire rack, set just above ½ to 1 inch of boiling water. Tightly cover the pan. Steaming is a popular way to prepare vegetables because it helps to preserve their texture, appearance, and nutrients.

Frying

Frying is cooking food in a fat, such as butter, margarine, cooking oil, shortening, lard, or meat drippings. The trick to frying is to have the fat hot enough that the food cooks without absorbing excessive grease, but not so hot that the fat begins to smoke or the food begins to burn.

Baking

Baking is a general term for cooking food by indirect dry heat. The food can be covered or uncovered and is usually in an oven or an oven-type appliance such as a toaster oven. When meat, except ham, is cooked in the oven by indirect dry heat, it is called roasting.

Broiling

Broiling is cooking food by direct, dry heat. Meat is broiled by placing it on a rack that allows the fat to drip away. Besides completely cooking foods, broiling can be used to brown or toast the tops of foods or melt ingredients such as cheese.

Savory Spaghetti Sauce

TIME:
15 minutes preparation
30 minutes cooking

EQUIPMENT:
large skillet   wooden spoon
knife   Dutch oven
dry measures   liquid measure
can opener   colander
measuring spoons

¾ **pound ground beef**
½ **cup chopped onion**

● Use your hands to crumble the ground beef into a large skillet. Stir in onion. Cook over medium heat, stirring occasionally, till the meat is brown and the onion is tender. Drain off fat.

---

1 **10¾-ounce can condensed tomato soup**
1 **8-ounce can tomato sauce**
½ **teaspoon dried oregano, crushed**
½ **teaspoon dried basil, crushed**
⅛ **teaspoon garlic powder**
Dash pepper

● Stir in the tomato soup, tomato sauce, crushed dried oregano, crushed dried basil, garlic powder, and pepper. Bring mixture to boiling. Reduce heat. Cover and simmer for 30 minutes, stirring occasionally.

---

3 **quarts water**
½ **teaspoon salt**
8 **ounces spaghetti**

● Meanwhile, in a Dutch oven or large kettle bring water and salt to a rolling boil. Add the spaghetti a little at a time so water does not stop boiling. Reduce heat slightly and continue boiling, uncovered, for 10 to 12 minutes or till the spaghetti is tender but still slightly firm. Stir occasionally. Drain the spaghetti in a colander.

Grated Parmesan cheese (optional)

● Serve the sauce atop the hot spaghetti. Top spaghetti with grated Parmesan cheese, if desired. Makes 4 main-dish servings.

You can test the doneness of pasta (spaghetti) two ways—the right way and the wrong way! You've probably already heard of the wrong way—throw the pasta against the wall. If it sticks to the wall, it is done. Not only does this method ruin your walls, it also gives you pasta that is overcooked.

The only way to know if pasta is cooked just right is to taste it. If the pasta is tender but still slightly firm and no longer tastes starchy, it's done. Immediately drain it to prevent further cooking.

If you need to keep the pasta warm for a short time, return it to the cooking pan, stir in a little butter or margarine, and cover it with a lid.

Chili

TIME:	EQUIPMENT:	
15 minutes preparation	large saucepan	colander
20 minutes cooking	knife	liquid measure
	dry measures	measuring spoons
	garlic press	ladle
	wooden spoon	soup bowls
	can opener	

After you've practiced making this easy Chili recipe a time or two, plan a chili supper for several of your friends. If you need to, you can make twice as much chili by doubling all the ingredients and cooking it in a Dutch oven instead of a large saucepan. Serve the chili with crusty French bread from a local bakery, an assortment of cheeses, and fresh or frozen fruit.

1 pound ground beef *or* ground pork
½ cup chopped onion
1 clove garlic, minced, *or* ⅛ teaspoon garlic powder

● Use your hands to crumble the ground beef or pork into a large saucepan. Stir in onion and garlic or garlic powder. Cook over medium heat till meat is browned, stirring occasionally. Drain off fat.

1 16-ounce can tomatoes, cut up
1 15½-ounce can red kidney beans, drained
½ cup beer *or* water
½ of a 6-ounce can (⅓ cup) tomato paste
2 to 3 teaspoons chili powder
½ teaspoon salt
½ teaspoon dried basil, crushed

● Stir in the *undrained* tomatoes, drained kidney beans, beer or water, tomato paste, chili powder, salt, and dried crushed basil. Bring to boiling. Reduce heat. Cover and simmer mixture for 20 minutes.

Chopped onion (optional)
Shredded cheddar cheese (optional)

● Ladle into soup bowls. Top with chopped onion and shredded cheddar cheese, if desired. Makes 4 to 6 main-dish servings.

Trademark Chili

Lots of cooks have their own trademark chili—a favorite chili recipe that they have personalized by changing it just a bit. All you have to do to personalize your chili is add a special ingredient to the chili recipe above. Try making it a spicier chili by adding one drained 4-ounce can of chopped green chili peppers when you add the tomatoes. Or, make the chili more colorful by adding ½ cup thinly sliced carrot or chopped green pepper when you cook the ground meat and onion. Another way you can individualize your chili is to change the kinds of toppers you serve. Instead of sprinkling the chili with cheese, dollop it with sour cream or top it with croutons, pumpkin seeds, chopped tomato, or sunflower nuts.

Pour the juices from the Dutch oven into a measuring cup. Spoon off the fat that rises to the top of the measuring cup.

To prevent lumps in your gravy, use a screw-top jar to thoroughly shake together the ½ cup water and the all-purpose flour.

Cook and stir the gravy till it is thickened and bubbly. To completely cook the flour, continue for 1 minute more.

Pot Roast and Gravy

TIME:
3 hours total preparation

EQUIPMENT:
knife
Dutch oven
measuring spoons
small bowl
liquid measure
wooden spoon

vegetable peeler
pancake turner
spoon
screw-top jar
dry measure

You can make pot roast that tastes like mom used to make! All you have to do is carefully follow this recipe. It takes you step by step to a perfectly done roast and delicious lump-free gravy.
Use water, wine, or beer to cook your pot roast. Gravy made from a roast cooked in water will taste rich and beefy. Gravy made from a roast cooked in wine or beer will have the extra zip that these spirits are famous for.

---

1 3- to 4-pound beef chuck pot roast 2 tablespoons cooking oil Pepper	● Use a sharp knife to trim excess fat from the pot roast. (Leave about ⅛ inch fat on the roast). Discard fat. In an oven-proof Dutch oven slowly brown the meat on both sides in the cooking oil over medium heat (allow about 10 minutes total time). Sprinkle with pepper.
¾ cup water, wine, *or* beer 1 tablespoon Worcestershire sauce 1½ teaspoons dried basil, thyme, marjoram, *or* oregano, crushed ½ teaspoon salt ⅛ teaspoon pepper	● In a small bowl stir together the ¾ cup water, wine, or beer; Worcestershire sauce; dried basil, dried thyme, dried marjoram, or dried oregano; salt; and ⅛ teaspoon pepper. Pour over the roast in the Dutch oven. Cover the roast and bake it in a 325° oven for 1 hour.
4 medium potatoes, peeled and quartered, *or* 16 whole new potatoes 4 medium carrots, cut into 1-inch lengths 4 stalks celery, bias-sliced into ½-inch pieces 2 medium onions, sliced and separated into rings	● If using new potatoes, peel a strip from around the center of each potato. Place potatoes, carrots, celery, and onions around and on top of the pot roast. Cover and bake in a 325° oven about 1½ to 1¾ hours or till the roast and vegetables are tender. Remove to a serving platter.
Water, wine, *or* beer	● For gravy (see tip, opposite), pour the juices from the Dutch oven into a measuring cup. Spoon off as much fat as possible. Measure the remaining juices and add additional water, wine, or beer, if necessary, to make 1½ cups total liquid. Return to Dutch oven.
½ cup cold water ¼ cup all-purpose flour Kitchen Bouquet (optional)	● In a screw-top jar shake together the ½ cup water and the flour. Stir into liquid in Dutch oven. Cook and stir over medium heat till thickened and bubbly. Cook and stir 1 minute more. If a darker gravy is desired, stir in a few drops of Kitchen Bouquet. Spoon some gravy over vegetables and meat. Pass remaining. Makes 8 main-dish servings.

Sweet 'n' Sour Meat Loaf

TIME:
15 minutes preparation
1¼ hours cooking

EQUIPMENT:

large bowl	wooden spoon
fork	can opener
liquid measure	knife
dry measures	pancake turner
measuring spoons	serving platter
shallow baking pan	spoon
small saucepan	

---

2 beaten eggs
¼ cup orange juice *or* milk
½ cup fine dry bread crumbs
2 tablespoons prepared mustard

● In a large bowl stir together the beaten eggs and orange juice or milk. Stir in the fine dry bread crumbs and prepared mustard.

1½ pounds ground beef

● Add the ground beef. Use your hands to thoroughly combine the mixture. Shape the meat mixture into an 8x4-inch loaf and place it in a shallow baking pan. Smooth the top of the meat mixture. Bake in a 350° oven about 1¼ hours or till the meat loaf is done.

¼ cup packed brown sugar
1 tablespoon cornstarch
½ teaspoon instant chicken bouillon granules
⅛ teaspoon ground ginger

● When meat loaf is almost done, in a small saucepan stir together the brown sugar, cornstarch, chicken bouillon granules, and ginger.

---

1 8-ounce can pineapple tidbits (juice pack)
1 medium green pepper, cut into 1-inch squares
2 tablespoons water
2 tablespoons vinegar
1 tablespoon soy sauce

● Stir in the *undrained* pineapple, green pepper squares, water, vinegar, and soy sauce. Cook and stir over medium heat till thickened and bubbly. Cook and stir 2 minutes more.

● Transfer meat loaf to a serving platter. Spoon the pineapple mixture over the meat loaf. Makes 6 main-dish servings.

Mixing a meat loaf is a project for those who don't mind getting their hands messy, because the best way to mix the ingredients is with your hands! You can use a spoon or fork to stir together the eggs, orange juice or milk, bread crumbs, and mustard. But after the meat is added, it is best to blend it all together with your hands so the ingredients are evenly distributed. Be careful not to get overly enthusiastic, because too much mixing will produce a meat loaf with a compact texture.

Shape a meat loaf as described in the recipe. Or, shape a loaf by spooning the meat mixture into an 8x4x2-inch loaf pan. Slightly press the meat mixture down around the edges, pulling it away from the sides of the pan. Bake either loaf in a 350° oven about 1¼ hours.

Scoring Steak

Unlike scoring in basketball, football, or hockey, you won't gain any points by scoring meat! But you will gain added flavor and tenderness. Scoring meat refers to using a knife to make shallow cuts on the surface of the meat. This shortens the meat fibers, making them more tender. And it allows the marinade to soak in, adding more flavor. For Marinated Steak, use a sharp knife to make long shallow cuts (about $\frac{1}{8}$ to $\frac{1}{4}$ inch deep) in a diamond pattern on both sides of the flank steak.

Marinated Steak

TIME: 6 hours advance preparation 15 minutes final preparation	EQUIPMENT: knife garlic press plastic bag broiler pan shallow baking dish tongs liquid measure spoon measuring spoons	Marinating steak is easier if you use a plastic bag. First place the steak in the bag, then set the bag in a shallow baking dish. Pour the marinade over the steak in the bag. Close the bag securely and turn it to distribute the marinade evenly over the meat. Be sure to turn the bag occasionally during the marinating period. Before broiling the steak, remove it from the marinade.
1 1- to 1½-pound beef flank steak	● Use a sharp knife to score steak at 1-inch intervals on both sides in a diamond pattern (see tip). Place steak in a plastic bag; set in a shallow baking dish.	
⅓ cup soy sauce 2 tablespoons water 2 tablespoons dry sherry 1 tablespoon cooking oil 2 cloves garlic, minced ½ teaspoon sugar ½ teaspoon ground ginger	● For marinade, stir together soy sauce, water, sherry, cooking oil, garlic, sugar, and ginger. Pour over the steak; close the bag. Chill in the refrigerator for 6 to 24 hours, turning the bag occasionally.	
	● Remove steak from bag. Drain steak well. Place steak on an unheated rack of a broiler pan. Broil 3 inches from the heat to desired doneness, turning once. (Allow 8 to 10 minutes total time for medium-rare.)	
	● To serve, slice meat diagonally across the grain into very thin slices. Spoon juices from the broiler pan over the meat. Makes 4 to 6 main-dish servings.	

Setting the Table

Don't stop at just preparing a wonderful meal. Make the meal more appetizing by setting an attractive table. Your plates and flatware don't have to be expensive or elegant; they can even be plastic or paper.

You can set a table any number of ways, and the fuss and frills need not confuse you. Keep your table setting simple. Arrange the plate in the center of each place setting. Then add the forks, knives, and spoons around the plate in the order they will be used, with the first items used to the outside. Forks are placed to the left of the plate. The knife and spoon go to the right of the plate, with the spoon on the outside and the knife, blade side in, next to the plate.

You can fold a napkin in almost any attractive manner and place it on the plate, to the left of the forks, or above the dinner plate, parallel to the edge of the table.

You can serve a salad on the same plate as the main dish, or on a salad plate. If you use a salad plate, place it directly above the forks.

If you use glasses and cups, place the glass at the tip of the knife and the cup to the right and lower than the glass. If a glass or cup is used alone, place it at the tip of the knife. After the meal, bring desserts to the table when the other dishes have been cleared.

Herbed Noodle Casserole

TIME: **45 minutes preparation** **20 minutes cooking**	EQUIPMENT:	
	large saucepan	can opener
	dry measures	liquid measure
	colander	shredder
	knife	kitchen shears
	measuring spoons	rubber spatula
	wooden spoon	1-quart casserole

The next time you do your grocery shopping, pick up the ingredients for Herbed Noodle Casserole. They'll all keep in the refrigerator, cupboard, or freezer for as long as a month. And then when you get in a bind and don't have dinner planned, you'll have everything you need to make a casserole.

1½ cups medium noodles 1 cup frozen cut broccoli	● In a large saucepan cook noodles according to package directions; drain in colander and set aside. In large saucepan cook broccoli according to package directions; drain and set aside.

¼ cup chopped onion 1 tablespoon butter *or* margarine 1 teaspoon all-purpose flour ½ teaspoon dried basil, oregano, *or* marjoram, crushed 1 7½-ounce can semi-condensed savory cream of mushroom soup ⅔ cup milk	● In the same large saucepan cook the onion in 1 tablespoon butter or margarine till tender. Stir in the flour and basil, oregano, or marjoram. Add the semi-condensed mushroom soup and milk all at once. Cook and stir over medium heat till thickened and bubbly. Cook and stir 1 minute more. Remove from heat.

½ cup shredded *process* Swiss *or* American cheese (2 ounces) 1 12½-ounce can tuna, drained; two 5-ounce cans chunk-style chicken; *or* one 15½-ounce can salmon, drained, flaked, and skin and bones removed 1 tablespoon snipped parsley	● Stir the cheese into the soup mixture till the cheese is melted. Gently stir in the tuna, chicken, or salmon. Add the parsley; stir till combined. 　Fold the cooked noodles and broccoli into the soup mixture by cutting down through the mixture with a rubber spatula. Scrape across the bottom of the saucepan, then bring the spatula up and over the mixture, close to the surface. Repeat this circular down-across-up-and-over motion till the soup mixture and noodles are combined. Transfer mixture into a 1-quart casserole.

By simply changing the ingredients, you can make the Herbed Noodle Casserole several times and it will never taste the same. For example, make it one time using oregano, Swiss cheese, and chicken. And the next time use basil, American cheese, and tuna. Your family and friends will never know that they are eating the same recipe!

1 tablespoon butter *or* margarine ¼ cup fine dry bread crumbs	● Melt 1 tablespoon butter or margarine. Toss with the bread crumbs. Sprinkle atop noodle mixture. Bake, uncovered, in a 350° oven for 20 to 25 minutes or till heated through. Makes 4 main-dish servings.

Cheesy Tamale Pie

TIME:
30 minutes preparation
20 minutes cooking

EQUIPMENT:

large skillet	can opener
knife	shredder
garlic press	1½-quart casserole
dry measures	medium bowl
measuring spoons	small bowl
wooden spoon	fork
	liquid measure

Spice up your life with a little Cheesy Tamale Pie! The mildly spicy flavor combination of chili peppers, garlic, onion, and sausage will remind you of a holiday in Mexico.

Be sure that the meat-tomato mixture is hot when the cornmeal mixture is spooned atop. Otherwise, the cornmeal mixture may remain doughy in the center.

---

1 pound bulk pork sausage
½ cup chopped onion
1 clove garlic, minced, *or* ⅛ teaspoon garlic powder

● Use your hands to crumble the sausage into a large skillet. Stir in the chopped onion and garlic. Cook over medium heat, stirring occasionally, till the meat is browned and the onion is tender. Drain off fat.

---

1 15-ounce can tomato sauce
1 4-ounce can green chili peppers, rinsed, seeded, and chopped
1 teaspoon dried oregano, crushed

● Stir in the tomato sauce, *half* of the chili peppers, and crushed dried oregano. Bring to boiling. Reduce heat. Simmer, uncovered, for 10 to 15 minutes or till meat-tomato mixture is very thick.

---

1 cup shredded American cheese (4 ounces)

● Add the shredded cheese, stirring till completely melted. Spoon mixture into an ungreased 1½-quart casserole.

½ cup all-purpose flour
½ cup yellow cornmeal
2 tablespoons sugar
2 teaspoons baking powder
¼ teaspoon salt

● In a medium bowl stir together the flour, yellow cornmeal, sugar, baking powder, and salt.

---

1 beaten egg
½ cup milk
2 tablespoons cooking oil

● In a small bowl combine the remaining chili peppers, egg, milk, and cooking oil; add to the cornmeal mixture. Stir just till moistened. Spoon atop the hot meat mixture.

● Bake, uncovered, in a 400° oven for 20 to 25 minutes or till done. Makes 6 main-dish servings.

Planning a Menu

Plan a menu? What's there to plan? You just throw two or three foods on the table and you're all set. Right? Wrong! Menu planning takes a little care to make eating healthy and enjoyable.

Start by considering nutrition. Not getting enough of the right foods can cause serious health problems. But you can avoid that by working within the guidelines of the five basic food groups.

Start first by planning two servings daily from the dairy products group. This can include foods such as milk, yogurt, ice cream, and cheese. You also need two servings daily of beef, lamb, pork, poultry, fish, shellfish, dry beans, eggs, or nuts—the protein-rich foods. The daily requirement for the breads and cereals food group is four servings daily of cereals, breads, crackers, pasta, rice, or grits. And finally you need four servings daily from the fruits and vegetables food group. This should include at least one dark-green or deep-yellow vegetable at least every other day.

After you meet the guidelines for the first four food groups you can include foods from the fifth group, the fats, sweets, and alcohol food group, if you want.

Now that you've got the nutritional aspects of menu planning figured out, consider how you can make the meal into an enjoyable eating experience. Not many people would like to eat all four servings from the breads and cereals food group in one meal. It's more pleasant to have a combination of types of foods. But how do you combine the foods? Start by

choosing a main course—this could be a meat for an evening meal or pancakes for a morning meal. If it's meat, you have fulfilled one serving from the protein-rich food group. And if it's pancakes, you've fulfilled one serving from the breads and cereals food group. Now you want to select foods from the other food groups to fulfill your remaining daily requirements as well as round out your meal.

Think about the flavor of your main course. For example, if it's spicy and hot chili, you probably want to select mild-flavored side dishes. Or, if it's a delicately seasoned fish, you should select side dishes that will not overpower its flavor.

Consider the temperature and texture of the foods you are going to serve. It's best to have some hot foods and some cold foods as well as some crisp foods and some soft foods. For example, hot spaghetti sauce is more appetizing with a cold, crisp salad than it is with hot buttered corn.

Also consider if the foods will look good together. This means thinking about the color and shapes of foods. An all-white meal of poached fish, mashed potatoes, bread, and milk is much less appetizing than a colorful meal of poached fish, buttered green beans, rye rolls, and fresh fruit compote. Also, a meal with everything the same shape, such as everything round or everything flat, will be much less interesting than a meal with varying shapes.

Easy Two-Crust Pizza

TIME:	EQUIPMENT:	
2 hours thawing	large skillet	ruler
45 minutes preparation	knife	pizza pan
25 minutes cooking	dry measures	spoon
	wooden spoon	pastry brush
	rolling pin	

1 16-ounce loaf frozen Italian, wheat, *or* white bread dough	● Let the frozen loaf of bread dough thaw completely according to the package directions.
¾ pound bulk Italian sausage *or* bulk pork sausage ¾ pound ground beef *or* ground pork ½ cup chopped onion ¼ cup chopped green pepper	● Meanwhile, crumble the sausage and the ground beef or pork into a large skillet. Add the chopped onion and chopped green pepper. Cook and stir over medium heat till the meat is browned and the onion and pepper are tender. Drain off fat.
All-purpose flour 2 tablespoons yellow cornmeal	● Set aside ⅓ of the bread dough. On a lightly floured surface roll the remaining bread dough into a 14-inch circle. (If dough becomes too elastic, let it stand a few minutes for easier rolling.) Grease a 12-inch pizza pan; sprinkle it with the cornmeal. Fit the dough into the pizza pan, pressing the edge of the dough just over the edge of the pan.
	● On a lightly floured surface roll the reserved ⅓ of the bread dough into a 14x8-inch rectangle. Cut into eight 14x1-inch strips; set aside.
12 ounces sliced mozzarella cheese ¾ cup grated Parmesan cheese (3 ounces) 1 4-ounce can sliced mushrooms, drained 1 15½-ounce jar (1½ cups) extra-thick spaghetti sauce	● Arrange *half* of the mozzarella cheese slices atop the circle of bread dough in the pizza pan. Spoon the meat mixture atop the mozzarella cheese. Top with the ¾ cup grated Parmesan cheese and drained, sliced mushrooms. Spoon the spaghetti sauce atop and top with remaining mozzarella cheese slices.
Milk Snipped parsley *or* grated Parmesan cheese	● Brush dough strips with milk; sprinkle with parsley or Parmesan. Use to make a lattice top on pizza, as instructed at right. Cut off excess dough beyond edges of pan. Pinch strips to edge to seal. Press edges toward center to hold in filling.
	● Bake in a 400° oven for 25 to 30 minutes or till crust is golden and filling is bubbly. Makes 8 main-dish servings.

Lattice-topped pizza is a specialty that your friends aren't likely to forget! What's more, the lattice top only looks as if it is hard to make. It's really very easy if you use this simplified version. Start by laying four strips of bread dough on the filled pizza all in one direction. Lay the remaining four strips across the first four at a 90-degree angle. Cut off the excess dough beyond the edges of the pizza pan, and pinch the edges of the lattice to the bottom crust to seal.

Stuffed Burgers

TIME:	EQUIPMENT:	
20 minutes preparation	large bowl	can opener
12 minutes cooking	fork	charcoal grill
	measuring spoons	pancake turner
	knife	

The mushrooms in these burgers add a delicious surprise to basic grilled burgers. And stuffing the burgers is easy to do. Just make patties that are ¼ inch thick or about half the thickness of regular hamburger patties. Spoon the mushrooms atop half of the patties, leaving about ½ inch at the edges of each patty uncovered. Top with the remaining thin hamburger patties. Use your fingers to press the edges of the patties together, sealing the mushrooms in the ground beef. If it's necessary, you can gently reshape the stuffed burgers to make them even.

1 beaten egg 3 tablespoons rolled oats 3 tablespoons sliced green onion 2 tablespoons catsup 1½ teaspoons prepared mustard ¾ teaspoon salt ⅛ teaspoon pepper 1½ pounds ground beef	● In a large bowl stir together the beaten egg, rolled oats, sliced green onion, catsup, prepared mustard, salt, and pepper. Add the ground beef. Use your hands to combine the mixture. Divide the meat mixture into 12 equal portions. Shape each into a ¼-inch-thick patty.
1 3-ounce can chopped mushrooms, drained	● Place mushrooms atop 6 of the patties to within ½ inch of the edges. Top with the remaining patties and press the edges together to seal.
6 slices American cheese (optional)	● Grill patties over *medium* coals to desired doneness, turning once. (Allow 12 to 15 minutes total time for medium doneness.) *Or,* place patties on rack of unheated broiler pan. Broil 3 inches from heat to desired doneness, turning once. (Allow 10 minutes total time for medium doneness.) Top patties with cheese and continue heating just till cheese melts, if desired.
6 hamburger buns, split and toasted 6 lettuce leaves (optional) 12 tomato slices (optional) Sliced onion (optional)	● Serve patties on buns with lettuce leaves, tomato slices, and sliced onion, if desired. Makes 6 main-dish servings.

Grilling Burgers

Our Stuffed Burgers are grilled over medium coals. If you're wondering what medium coals are, here's an easy way to tell. Hold your hand just above the hot coals at the height where the burgers will be cooking. Then count the seconds you can hold your hand there. If your hand gets too hot after 3 seconds, the coals are medium-hot; after 4 seconds, the coals are medium.

Ham with Pineapple-Orange Sauce

TIME:
15 minutes preparation
40 minutes cooking

EQUIPMENT:
knife
rack
shallow baking pan
shredder
measuring spoons
small bowl
can opener
colander
liquid measure
medium saucepan
wooden spoon

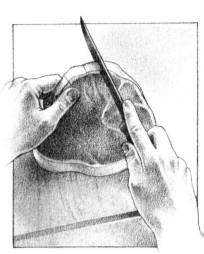

Unless you want your ham slice to resemble a bowl after it's baked, be sure to slash the edges. Cutting ¼-inch-deep slashes at 1-inch intervals around the ham slice will keep the ham from curling while it's baking.

1 2-pound fully cooked ham center slice, cut ¾ inch thick	● Use a sharp knife to cut slashes about ¼ inch deep and 1 inch apart around the edge of the ham slice. Place the ham slice on a rack in a shallow baking pan. Bake in a 350° oven about 30 minutes or till heated through.
2 oranges	● Meanwhile, finely shred ¼ teaspoon orange peel; set aside. Cut the remaining peel and white membrane off the oranges; discard. Work over a small bowl and remove the orange sections by cutting into the center of the fruit between one section and the membrane. Then turn the knife and slide it down the other side of the section next to the membrane. Remove and discard any seeds. Repeat with remaining sections. Set the orange sections aside. Reserve the juice in the bowl.
1 8-ounce can pineapple chunks (juice pack) Orange juice *or* pineapple juice	● Drain the pineapple, reserving the juice. Stir the orange juice and pineapple juice together and add enough additional orange or pineapple juice to make 1 cup total fruit juice mixture.
4 teaspoons cornstarch **¼ teaspoon ground cinnamon**	● In a medium saucepan stir together cornstarch, cinnamon, and orange peel. Add the 1 cup fruit juice mixture. Cook and stir over medium heat till the mixture is thickened and bubbly. Cook and stir 2 minutes more. Stir in the orange sections and pineapple chunks. Pour fruit sauce over ham. Cover and bake 10 minutes more. Makes 8 main-dish servings.

Stroganoff-Style Round Steak

TIME:	EQUIPMENT:	
1¾ hours total preparation	knife	wooden spoon
	cutting board	tongs
	custard cup	foil
	measuring spoons	dry measures
	meat mallet	Dutch oven
	10-inch skillet	kitchen shears
	liquid measure	

Beef Stroganoff is the name of a main dish that includes strips of beef and a sauce composed of sour cream and a variety of seasonings. It was named after the gourmet, Count P. Stroganoff, a nineteenth-century Russian diplomat. Stroganoff-Style Round Steak gets its name from the sauce, which uses the same flavorings as Beef Stroganoff.

1 ¾-pound beef round steak, cut ¾ inch thick 4 teaspoons all-purpose flour ½ teaspoon salt ⅛ teaspoon pepper	● Trim fat from the meat; remove any bone. Cut into 4 serving-size pieces. In a custard cup combine 4 teaspoons flour, ½ teaspoon salt, and pepper. Sprinkle about *half* of the flour mixture over one side of the meat pieces. Use a meat mallet to pound the meat from the center to the outside edges. Turn meat over; sprinkle with the remaining flour mixture and pound with a meat mallet.
1 tablespoon cooking oil ¾ cup water 1 small onion, sliced 1 teaspoon instant beef bouillon granules ¼ teaspoon dried oregano *or* basil, crushed	● In a heavy 10-inch skillet heat the oil. Add the meat to the skillet and brown quickly on both sides. Remove from heat. Stir in the water, onion, bouillon granules, and oregano or basil. Cover and cook over low heat about 1¼ hours or till the meat is tender.
4 teaspoons all-purpose flour ½ cup dairy sour cream *or* plain yogurt	● For sauce, remove the meat from the skillet. Cover the meat with foil. Pour meat juices from the skillet into a glass measure. Use a spoon to skim off fat. Measure ¾ cup juices (if necessary, add water to equal ¾ cup liquid). Return juice mixture to skillet. Stir 4 teaspoons flour into the sour cream or yogurt. Stir into the juice mixture. Cook and stir over medium heat till thickened and bubbly. Cook and stir 1 minute more.
6 cups water ¼ teaspoon salt 4 ounces noodles Snipped parsley (optional)	● Meanwhile, in a Dutch oven bring the water and salt to a boil. Add the noodles a few at a time, stirring constantly. Cook noodles in boiling salted water for 8 to 10 minutes or till tender. Drain. Top noodles with meat and sauce. If desired, sprinkle with parsley. Makes 4 main-dish servings.

To avoid having a curdled sauce over your Stroganoff-Style Round Steak, be sure to stir the flour into the sour cream before you add it to the meat juices. This helps to stabilize the sour cream.

Crush cornflakes or corn
squares by putting some
cereal in a plastic bag.
Press out most of the air
and tightly close the bag.
Now press the bag with
your fist or hands till the
cereal is crushed.

Oven Fried Chicken

TIME:	EQUIPMENT:	
15 minutes preparation	paper toweling	waxed paper
1 hour cooking	small bowl	pastry brush
	small saucepan	dry measures
	measuring spoons	shallow baking pan

Do you like fried chicken, but hate to clean up the spattered grease left by frying? If so, Oven Fried Chicken is for you. It tastes like fried chicken, but is made in the oven, which means you won't have to watch the chicken or clean up any spattered grease.

1 2½- to 3-pound broiler-fryer chicken, cut up	● Rinse chicken pieces with water; pat dry with paper toweling.
3 tablespoons butter *or* margarine, melted 1½ teaspoons dried basil *or* marjoram, crushed ½ teaspoon salt	● In a small bowl combine the melted butter or margarine, dried basil or marjoram, salt, and ¼ teaspoon *pepper.* Use a pastry brush to brush the chicken pieces with the butter mixture.
2½ cups cornflakes, crushed, *or* bite-size shredded corn squares crushed Parsley sprigs	● Roll chicken in cornflakes or corn squares. Place, skin side up, in an ungreased shallow baking pan so pieces aren't touching each other. Bake in a 375° oven about 1 hour or till tender. *Do not* turn. Garnish with parsley sprigs, if desired. Makes 6 main-dish servings.

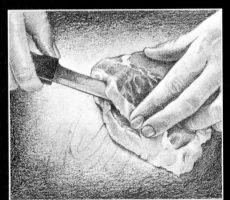
Use a sharp knife to cut a 1½- to 2-inch-long slit in the fatty side of the chop. Insert knife into the slit and draw it from side to side to form a pocket.

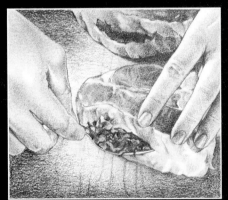
Using a tablespoon, lightly spoon about ¼ cup of the stuffing into the pocket of each pork chop. The stuffing should not be tightly packed.

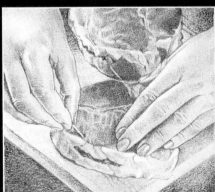
Securely close the pocket opening with 1 or 2 wooden picks inserted diagonally. This keeps the stuffing from falling out while the chops broil.

Cutting Pockets

A Better Homes and Gardens Test Kitchen home economist, Kay, recommends using a sharp knife with a long, thin blade (a boning knife) to cut pockets in the pork chops. "Start by using the knife to cut a 1½- to 2-inch-long slit in the fatty side of the chop," says Kay. "Then insert the knife into the slit and draw it from one side to the other to form a larger pocket inside the chop. The resulting pocket should go from one side of the chop to the other and almost all the way to the bone."

Pine Nut-Stuffed Pork Chops

TIME:
20 minutes preparation
22 minutes cooking

EQUIPMENT:

small skillet	measuring spoons
shredder	spoon
dry measures	wooden picks
knife	broiler pan
small bowl	tongs

Place the stuffed pork chops on the rack of an unheated broiler pan. (Using an unheated pan keeps the chops from sticking to the surface.) Use a ruler to measure the distance from the broiler element to the surface of the chops, making sure the distance is 4 to 5 inches.

---

1 cup shredded carrot
½ cup pine nuts *or* slivered almonds
¼ cup sliced green onion
2 tablespoons butter *or* margarine

● In a small skillet cook the shredded carrot, pine nuts or almonds, and sliced green onion in the butter or margarine till the carrot and onion are tender.

---

4 pork loin rib chops, cut 1 inch thick
1 teaspoon dried savory *or* marjoram, crushed
½ teaspoon dried basil, crushed
¼ teaspoon salt
⅛ teaspoon pepper

● Use a sharp knife to cut a pocket in each chop by cutting from the fat side of the chop almost to the bone edge.
   In a small bowl combine the savory or marjoram, basil, salt, and pepper. Rub the herb mixture on all surfaces of the meat and inside the pockets.
   Spoon the carrot mixture into the pork chop pockets. Securely fasten pocket openings with wooden picks.

● Place the stuffed pork chops on the unheated rack of a broiler pan. Broil 4 to 5 inches from heat for 12 minutes. Turn chops and broil for 10 to 12 minutes more or till the chops are done. Makes 4 main-dish servings.

Sausage Tropicana

TIME:
20 minutes preparation
40 minutes cooking

EQUIPMENT:

medium saucepan	large skillet
liquid measure	knife
dry measures	can opener
measuring spoons	small bowl
wooden spoon	

This easy one-dish meal is not only delicious, it's also attractive. Serve it at your next dinner party, along with a vegetable salad, dinner rolls, and your favorite beverage. Then end the meal with an easy dessert, such as ice cream.

1½ **cups water**
⅔ **cup brown rice**
½ **teaspoon salt**

● In a medium saucepan stir together water, brown rice, and salt. Cover with a tight-fitting lid; bring to boiling. Reduce heat. Simmer, covered, for 40 to 50 minutes or till water is absorbed. (Rice will be chewy.)

---

1 **pound fully cooked Polish sausage, cut into ¼-inch-thick slices**
1 **large onion, thinly sliced and separated into rings**
1 **green pepper, cut into 1-inch squares**
2 **tablespoons cooking oil**

● Meanwhile, in a large skillet cook the Polish sausage slices, onion rings, and green pepper squares in hot cooking oil till the onion is tender, stirring frequently. Drain off fat.

---

1 **16-ounce can peach slices**
2 **tablespoons sweet pickle relish**

● Stir *undrained* peaches and the pickle relish into the sausage mixture. Bring to boiling, stirring occasionally. Reduce heat. Cover and simmer mixture for 5 minutes.

If you don't have cornstarch on hand, you also can thicken mixtures with all-purpose flour. Just substitute twice as much all-purpose flour for the cornstarch. In Sausage Tropicana, for example, use 2 tablespoons all-purpose flour instead of the 1 tablespoon cornstarch.

¼ **cup cold water**
1 **tablespoon cornstarch**
2 **teaspoons prepared mustard**
½ **teaspoon instant chicken bouillon granules**
  Dash pepper

● In a small bowl stir together the cold water and cornstarch. Stir in the mustard, bouillon granules, and pepper. Stir into the sausage mixture in the skillet. Cook and stir over medium heat till thickened and bubbly. Cook and stir 2 minutes more. Serve over hot cooked brown rice. Makes 4 main-dish servings.

Tarragon-Sauced Chicken Breasts

TIME:
30 minutes preparation
15 minutes cooking

EQUIPMENT:

medium saucepan	knife
liquid measure	clear plastic wrap
dry measures	meat mallet
measuring spoons	large skillet
wooden spoon	fork
kitchen shears	oven-proof platter

An important step in making Tarragon-Sauced Chicken Breasts is pounding the chicken breasts till they are slightly flattened. Start by placing a boned and skinned chicken breast half between two layers of clear plastic wrap to prevent perforating the chicken. Using the fine-tooth side of a meat mallet, pound each piece of chicken till it is slightly flattened, working from the center to the edges. If you do not have a meat mallet, you also can use the flat side of a chef's knife or a cleaver.

---

2 cups cold water
1 cup long grain rice
1 tablespoon butter *or* margarine
1 teaspoon salt
¼ cup snipped parsley

● In a medium saucepan stir together the water, rice, 1 tablespoon butter or margarine, and salt. Cover with a tight-fitting lid. Bring to boiling; reduce heat. Cook for 15 minutes; *do not* lift cover. Remove from heat. Let stand, covered, for 10 minutes. Stir in parsley.

---

2 whole large chicken breasts, skinned, halved lengthwise, and boned
1 teaspoon lemon juice
2 tablespoons sliced green onion
2 tablespoons butter *or* margarine

● Meanwhile, place each chicken breast half between 2 pieces of clear plastic wrap. With a meat mallet, pound out from center to flatten slightly. Remove plastic wrap. Rub each chicken breast half with some of the lemon juice. Sprinkle lightly with salt and pepper.

In a large skillet cook the green onion in the 2 tablespoons butter or margarine till tender but not brown. Add chicken. Cook 3 minutes per side or till tender. Remove to an oven-proof serving platter. Keep warm in a 200° oven.

---

2 teaspoons all-purpose flour
¼ teaspoon dried tarragon, crushed
Dash pepper *or* white pepper
1 cup light cream *or* milk

● Stir the flour, dried tarragon, and pepper or white pepper into the skillet drippings. Add the light cream or milk all at once. Cook and stir over medium heat till the mixture is thickened and bubbly. Cook and stir 1 minute more.

---

1 slightly beaten egg yolk

● Stir *half* of the hot mixture into the egg yolk. Return all of the mixture to the saucepan. Cook and stir over low heat for 2 minutes. Serve chicken atop rice. Spoon sauce over chicken. Makes 4 main-dish servings.

Sherry-Sauced Fish

TIME:
20 minutes preparation
18 minutes cooking

EQUIPMENT:
pastry brush
measuring spoons
small saucepan
wooden picks
broiler pan
fork
medium saucepan
knife

dry measures
garlic press
wooden spoon
small bowl
platter
spoon

If you've ever been served undercooked or overcooked fish, you may be reluctant to try cooking fish yourself. Don't be. It's really easy to tell when fish reaches the proper degree of doneness. All you have to do is cook the fish for the minimum amount of time. Insert the tines of a table fork into the fish at a 45-degree angle and twist the fork gently. If the fish flakes, it is done perfectly. If it resists flaking and still has a translucent quality, it is not done and should be broiled a little longer. If it is dry and mealy, you have cooked the fish too long.

4 4-ounce fresh or frozen fish fillets
2 tablespoons butter or margarine, melted
Paprika

● Thaw fish, if frozen. Using a pastry brush, brush fish fillets with *half* of the 2 tablespoons melted butter or margarine. Sprinkle with paprika. Roll up fish, starting with narrow end; secure with wooden picks.

● Place on a rack in an unheated broiler pan. Brush tops with some of the remaining melted butter or margarine. Broil fish 4 inches from heat for 10 minutes. Carefully turn fish; brush with remaining melted butter or margarine. Broil for 8 to 10 minutes longer or till fish flakes easily when tested with a fork.

1 cup sliced fresh mushrooms
¼ cup chopped onion
1 small clove garlic, minced
1 tablespoon butter or margarine

● Meanwhile, in a medium saucepan cook mushrooms, onion, and minced garlic in the 1 tablespoon butter or margarine over medium heat till tender.

¼ cup dairy sour cream
1 tablespoon all-purpose flour
½ cup chicken broth
1 tablespoon dry sherry

● In a small bowl combine sour cream and flour. Stir in broth. Add to the mushroom mixture. Cook and stir over medium heat till thickened and bubbly. Cook and stir 1 minute more. Stir in sherry; heat through.

● Place the fish on a serving platter. Spoon some sauce atop the fish. Pass remainder. Makes 4 main-dish servings.

Fish Newburg

TIME: 15 minutes preparation 10 minutes cooking	EQUIPMENT: knife fork large skillet colander liquid measure saucepan measuring spoons wooden spoon dry measures toaster	Make toast points for Fish Newburg by toasting 4 slices of bread. Diagonally cut each slice in half so that you have large triangles. Cut each large triangle in half again so you have 16 small triangles out of the 4 slices of toasted bread.
1 **pound fresh** *or* **frozen fish fillets** ½ **cup water** 1 **teaspoon instant chicken bouillon granules** ¼ **cup sliced green onion**	● Thaw fish, if frozen. Cut fish fillets into 1-inch pieces. In a large skillet stir together water and bouillon granules. Bring to boiling. Add fish pieces and onion. Reduce heat. Cover and simmer for 6 to 8 minutes or till the fish flakes easily when tested with a fork. Drain the fish and onion, reserving ½ *cup* of the liquid. Set aside.	
2 **teaspoons cornstarch** ½ **teaspoon salt** **Dash ground red pepper** 1 **cup milk**	● In a saucepan stir together cornstarch, salt, and ground red pepper. Add the milk all at once. Stir in the reserved liquid from the fish. Cook and stir over medium heat till thickened and bubbly. Cook and stir 2 minutes more.	
¼ **cup dry sherry** 2 **tablespoons tomato paste**	● Stir together the sherry and tomato paste. Add to the mixture in the saucepan. Gently stir in the fish-onion mixture. Heat through.	
4 **slices bread, toasted and quartered**	● Serve fish mixture over toast points. Makes 4 main-dish servings.	

Buying Fish Fillets

If you are purchasing fresh fish fillets, look for fillets that have a fresh appearance, with no drying out around the edges. Fish smells sweet and not "fishy," the flesh of the fish is firm and elastic, and the flesh springs back when you lightly press on it.

If a retailer is careless, frozen fish may thaw and freeze repeatedly before you buy it, causing a loss of flavor and a risk of spoilage. So when you purchase frozen fish, avoid any packages that have these signs of thawing and refreezing: packages that are misshapen, packages that have torn wrappers, or packages that have frost or blood visible.

Dinner Party

With a little planning, you can prepare an elegant dinner party for six and feel confident that it'll be a hit. Start by doing as much as you can before the party, such as setting the table and chilling the wine. Then, up to 4 hours before serving time, prepare and chill a simple tossed salad and an easy dessert. An hour and a half before serving time, start preparing Honey and Pepper Chicken. As soon as the chicken is in the oven, slice the onion and shred the carrot for the pilaf so they will be ready to go. Prepare the coffee. Put the pilaf ingredients together about 45 minutes before the chicken is due to come out of the oven. Place the pilaf in the oven along with the chicken. Now all you have to do is relax and greet your dinner guests! (Turn to pages 40 and 41 for recipes.)

MENU

Honey and Pepper Chicken
Oven Rice Pilaf
Tossed salad
Coffee
Easy dessert

Honey and Pepper Chicken

TIME:
10 minutes preparation
50 minutes cooking

EQUIPMENT:

paper toweling	small bowl
rack	liquid measure
shallow baking pan	pastry brush
small saucepan	tongs
measuring spoons	serving platter
wooden spoon	

The spicy flavor of Honey and Pepper Chicken comes from peppercorns, which are the whole dried berries from the black pepper vine. You can buy them in the spice section of your grocery store. For cracked peppercorns, either buy them cracked or buy them whole and crack them yourself.

3 whole large chicken breasts, halved lengthwise
1 tablespoon butter _or_ margarine, melted
1 to 1½ teaspoons cracked peppercorns
¾ teaspoon ground ginger
½ teaspoon salt

● Rinse chicken pieces. Pat dry with paper toweling. Place chicken, skin side up, on a rack in a shallow baking pan. Stir together the butter or margarine, cracked peppercorns, ginger, and salt. Use your hands to rub mixture over the surfaces of the chicken pieces. Bake in a 375° oven for 30 minutes.

¼ cup honey
2 tablespoons soy sauce

● In a small bowl stir together the honey and soy sauce. Using a pastry brush, brush some over the chicken pieces. Continue baking about 20 minutes more or till the chicken is tender, brushing occasionally with more of the honey mixture. Transfer to a serving platter. Makes 6 main-dish servings.

MENU COUNTDOWN
4 Hours Ahead:
Prepare and chill tossed salad.
Prepare easy dessert.
1½ Hours Ahead:
Prepare Honey and Pepper Chicken; place in oven.
Slice onion and shred carrot for Oven Rice Pilaf.
Prepare coffee, if desired.
45 Minutes Ahead:
Prepare Oven Rice Pilaf; place in oven.
15 Minutes Ahead:
Open wine, if desired.

Easy Desserts

Desserts don't have to take hours of work to be both attractive and delicious. For an easy but elegant dessert, scoop layers of different flavors of ice cream, such as chocolate and cherry, chocolate and vanilla, vanilla and strawberry, peach and peppermint, or chocolate and peppermint, into parfait glasses. Then serve them with fancy purchased cookies. Here's another simple dessert idea: Stir 2 to 3 tablespoons of your favorite liqueur, such as brandy or Amaretto, into a cup of coffee and top it with whipped cream. Or, buy a chocolate truffle for each guest and pass the truffles in a pretty candy dish for a dessert.

Making Coffee

To make six cups of coffee, use 4½ cups *water* and 6 to 12 tablespoons *ground coffee,* depending on how strong you like your coffee. For percolator coffee, pour the water into a percolator; stand the stem and basket in the pot. Measure the coffee into the basket. Add the basket lid; cover the pot. Bring water to boiling; reduce heat and perk for 5 to 8 minutes. Let stand for 1 to 2 minutes; remove the basket. Keep warm over low heat. For drip coffee, measure the coffee into the basket. Pour boiling water over coffee. When the coffee is finished dripping, remove basket and discard grounds. For electric drip coffee makers, follow the manufacturer's directions.

Oven Rice Pilaf

TIME:
15 minutes preparation
35 minutes cooking

EQUIPMENT:
medium saucepan
liquid measure
measuring spoons
wooden spoon
1½-quart casserole
dry measures
shredder
knife
fork

Although thousands of rice varieties are available, they generally are classified into three main categories—long grain, medium grain, and short grain rice. The grains of long grain rice, used in Oven Rice Pilaf, are about four times as long as they are wide.

2¼ cups water
1 tablespoon butter *or* margarine
1 tablespoon instant chicken bouillon granules
1 teaspoon dried thyme, crushed

● In a medium saucepan stir together the water, butter or margarine, instant chicken bouillon granules, and crushed dried thyme. Bring bouillon mixture to boiling. Pour into an ungreased 1½-quart casserole.

1 cup long grain rice
1 cup shredded carrot
¼ cup sliced green onion

● Immediately stir in rice, carrot, and onion. Cover tightly. Bake in a 375° oven for 35 minutes. Remove from oven. Let stand for 15 minutes. Fluff with a fork. Makes 6 side-dish servings.

French Omelets

TIME: **18 minutes preparation** **8 minutes cooking**	EQUIPMENT: small bowl pancake turner measuring spoons spoon fork oven-proof plate 6-inch skillet
Omelet filling (see recipes, below and right) **4 eggs** **2 tablespoons water** **¼ teaspoon salt** **Dash pepper**	● Prepare desired omelet filling. Set aside. In a small bowl beat together the eggs, water, salt, and pepper with a fork till combined but not frothy.
1 tablespoon cooking oil	● In a 6- or 8-inch skillet with flared sides heat *half* of the oil. Lift and tilt the pan to coat the sides. Add *half* of the egg mixture; cook over medium heat. As eggs set, run a pancake turner around the edge of the skillet, lifting eggs to allow uncooked portion to flow underneath. When eggs are set but still shiny, remove pan from the heat.
	● Spoon *half* of the desired filling across the center of the omelet. Fold one-third of the omelet atop filling. Overlap the remaining one-third over center. Slide the filled omelet from pan onto oven-proof plate. Keep warm in a 200° oven while preparing second omelet.
Fresh basil leaves (optional)	● To make second omelet, repeat cooking using the remaining oil, egg mixture, and desired omelet filling. Garnish omelets with basil leaves, if desired. Makes 2 main-dish servings.

You don't have to be a French chef to prepare French omelets! It just takes a little know-how to get you through the tricky steps. The first problem you may encounter is knowing when the oil in the skillet is hot enough to add the eggs. You can test it by adding a drop or two of water. If the water sizzles and hops across the surface, the skillet is ready. Be careful though, you don't want to get the skillet so hot that the oil begins to smoke.

Then, as the eggs begin to set, run a pancake turner or metal spatula around the edge of the skillet, lifting the eggs to allow the uncooked portion to flow underneath. If you like, you can tip the pan slightly so the eggs flow easier. Don't stir the egg mixture at this point or you could end up with scrambled eggs.

Country Omelet Filling

TIME: **15 minutes total preparation**	EQUIPMENT: knife
½ of an 8-ounce package brown and serve sausages, sliced	● In a small skillet cook the sliced sausage just till it begins to brown. Remove from heat. Drain off fat.
1 large orange, peeled	● Section orange over skillet (see directions, page 28), allowing juice to drop into skillet. Stir orange sections into mixture in skillet. Heat through.

For a one-dish breakfast, use the Country Omelet Filling in your omelet. It gives you a winning breakfast combination of eggs, sausage, and oranges.

Curry Omelet Filling:
Cook 2 tablespoons sliced
green onion in 1
tablespoon *butter or
margarine* till tender. Stir
in 1 tablespoon all-
purpose *flour,* ½ teaspoon
curry powder, ⅛ teaspoon
salt, and a dash *pepper.*
Add ⅓ cup *milk* all at
once. Cook and stir till
thickened and bubbly.
Cook and stir 1 minute
more. Gently stir in ¼ cup
chopped *tomato,* ¼ cup
chopped *peanuts,* and 2
tablespoons *raisins.*

*Mushroom and Tomato
Omelet Filling:* Melt 2
tablespoons *butter or
margarine* in a small
skillet. Stir in ½ teaspoon
crushed dried *basil.* Add
⅔ cup sliced fresh
mushrooms. Cook and stir
till the mushrooms are
tender. Stir in 1 cup
chopped *tomato.*

*Ham and Cheddar
Omelet Filling:* Cook 2
tablespoons sliced *green
onion* in 1 tablespoon
butter or margarine till
tender. Stir in 1
tablespoon all-purpose
flour and a dash *pepper.*
Add ½ cup *milk* all at
once. Cook and stir till
thickened and bubbly.
Cook and stir 1 minute
more. Stir in ½ cup
shredded *cheddar cheese*
and ½ cup cubed fully
cooked *ham* till the
cheese is melted.

**French Omelet with
Mushroom and Tomato
Omelet Filling**

Weekend Brunch

IT'S THE WEEKEND! You want to make a special brunch, but you don't want a lot of hassle. It's no problem with our weekend special. Just make the delicious Eggs in a Puff—it's really scrambled eggs and vegetables in a cream-puff bowl. Then serve it with refreshing Champagne Sipper. Turn to pages 46 and 47 for the recipes.

MENU

Eggs in a Puff
Champagne Sipper

Eggs in a Puff

TIME:
30 minutes preparation
30 minutes cooking

EQUIPMENT:

medium saucepan	bowl
liquid measure	fork
wooden spoon	large skillet
dry measures	shredder
measuring spoons	pancake turner
9-inch pie plate	spoon

When making Eggs in a Puff, be sure to cool the hot flour-butter mixture for 5 minutes before adding the eggs. This slight cooling prevents the eggs from cooking before they can be blended into the flour-butter mixture. Add the eggs, one at a time, beating after each addition of an egg till the mixture is smooth.

---

1 cup boiling water
½ cup butter *or* margarine
1 cup all-purpose flour
¼ teaspoon salt

● Preheat oven to 400°. To make the puff, in a medium saucepan stir together the boiling water and the ½ cup butter or margarine till the butter is melted. Add·the flour and ¼ teaspoon salt all at once; stir vigorously. Cook and stir over medium heat till the mixture forms a ball that doesn't separate. Remove from heat; cool mixture for 5 minutes.

---

4 eggs

● Add the 4 eggs, one at a time, beating after each till smooth. Spread the batter over the bottom and up the sides of a greased 9-inch pie plate. Bake in a 400° oven for 30 to 35 minutes or till golden brown and puffy.

---

8 beaten eggs
⅓ cup milk *or* light cream
¼ teaspoon salt
⅛ teaspoon pepper
1 6-ounce package frozen pea pods, diagonally halved, *or* 1 cup frozen peas

● Meanwhile, in a bowl use a fork to stir together the 8 beaten eggs, the milk or light cream, ¼ teaspoon salt, and pepper. Stir in the pea pods or peas.

MENU COUNTDOWN
Several Days Ahead:
Chill champagne.
45 Minutes Ahead:
Prepare puff for Eggs in a Puff.
Prepare fruit cup, if desired.
20 Minutes Ahead:
Prepare eggs for Eggs in a Puff.
Prepare Champagne Sipper.

---

2 tablespoons butter *or* margarine
½ cup shredded Swiss cheese
½ cup cooked chopped ham

● Heat the 2 tablespoons butter or margarine in a large skillet just till hot enough to make a drop of water sizzle. Pour in egg mixture. Reduce heat to low. When the egg mixture starts to set on the bottom and sides of the skillet, sprinkle with the ½ cup Swiss cheese and ham. Lift and fold the egg mixture with a pancake turner till eggs are cooked and cheese is melted.

¼ cup shredded Swiss cheese

● Spoon the cooked eggs into the baked puff. Sprinkle with the ¼ cup Swiss cheese. Cut into wedges to serve. Makes 6 main-dish servings.

Champagne Sipper

TIME:	EQUIPMENT:	
5 minutes preparation	large pitcher	wooden spoon
	liquid measure	glasses

1 375-ml bottle champagne, chilled

2 cups lemonade *or* orange juice

Whole fresh *or* frozen strawberries

● In a large pitcher stir together champagne and lemonade or orange juice. Pour into glasses. Garnish with whole fresh or frozen strawberries. Makes 6 (¾-cup) servings.

Fruit Cups

One of the easiest ways to make fruit cups is to simply purchase either frozen mixed fruit or canned chunky mixed fruit and spoon it into the dessert dishes. But you also can make your own combinations of fruit. Try mixing frozen strawberries and canned pineapple tidbits; fresh orange sections and canned pineapple chunks; canned peaches and frozen blueberries; fresh banana slices and frozen strawberries; canned sweet cherries and frozen peaches; or any other combination.

If you use canned fruit in your fruit cup, place the unopened cans of fruit in your refrigerator the day before you plan to serve brunch. Then when you open the cans and mix the fruit on the morning of the brunch, the fruit will already be nicely chilled.

Stuffed French Toast

| TIME:
20 minutes preparation
20 minutes cooking | EQUIPMENT:
mixer bowl   butter knife
measuring spoons   small bowl
electric mixer   liquid measure
rubber spatula   electric skillet
dry measures   pancake turner
knife   small saucepan | Surprise your family by making something familiar, yet different, for breakfast or brunch this weekend—Stuffed French Toast. It's familiar because the bread is dipped and fried just like ordinary French toast. And it's different because it's stuffed with a delicious cream cheese and nut filling. |

1 8-ounce package cream cheese, softened 1 teaspoon vanilla ½ cup chopped walnuts	● In a small mixer bowl beat the cream cheese and vanilla on medium speed of an electric mixer till fluffy. Stir in chopped walnuts.
1 16-ounce loaf French bread	● Cut the French bread into ten to twelve 1½-inch-thick slices. Cut a pocket in the top of each slice (*see tip, opposite*). Fill *each* pocket with about *1½ tablespoons* of the cheese mixture.
4 beaten eggs 1 cup whipping cream ½ teaspoon vanilla ½ teaspoon ground nutmeg	● In a small bowl stir together the eggs, whipping cream, vanilla, and nutmeg. Dip bread slices in egg mixture, being careful not to squeeze out filling. Cook in a lightly greased electric skillet or griddle till golden brown, turning once. Keep cooked slices hot in a 200° oven while cooking the remainder.
1 12-ounce jar apricot preserves ½ cup orange juice	● Meanwhile, in a small saucepan heat together the apricot preserves and orange juice, stirring frequently. To serve, drizzle apricot sauce over the hot French toast. Makes 10 to 12 stuffed slices.

1 Cut a pocket in the top of each bread slice by using the point of a sharp knife to cut from the top almost to the bottom of the slice. Cut across the top of the slice, but do not cut the sides of the slice. Fill each pocket with cream cheese mixture.

2 Dip the filled bread slices in the egg mixture, being careful not to squeeze out the cream cheese mixture. Be sure to dip both sides of the bread slice.

3 Cook the filled bread slices in a lightly greased electric skillet or griddle till both sides are golden brown, turning once.

1 Cut the shortening into the flour mixture till the mixture resembles coarse crumbs. The best utensils to use for cutting in shortening are a pastry blender or two knives. Mixing by hand tends to soften the shortening, making a sticky, difficult-to-handle dough.

2 Gently push the flour-shortening mixture against the edges of the bowl, making a well. Add the milk all at once, pouring it into the well.

3 Using a fork, stir the mixture quickly. Stir just till the mixture follows the fork around the bowl and forms a soft dough.

4 Turn the dough out onto a lightly floured surface. Knead gently for 10 to 12 strokes (see tip at right). This helps to develop the biscuit's structure and distributes the moisture to make the biscuits more flaky.

5 On the lightly floured surface pat the dough to ½-inch thickness (or use a lightly floured rolling pin). Sprinkle the dough with a little flour, if necessary, to keep the dough from sticking.

6 Cut the dough with a 2½-inch biscuit cutter or a 2½-inch-wide glass. Dip the cutter in flour between cuts to prevent sticking. Press the cutter straight down to get evenly shaped biscuits. Transfer the biscuits to an ungreased baking sheet.

Cheese-Herb Biscuits

TIME: 20 minutes preparation 10 minutes cooking	EQUIPMENT: large bowl liquid measure dry measures fork measuring spoons biscuit cutter wooden spoon baking sheet pastry blender

2 **cups all-purpose flour**
1 **tablespoon baking powder**
2 **teaspoons sugar**
½ **teaspoon dried oregano,**
     basil, savory, or
     marjoram, crushed
½ **teaspoon cream of tartar**
¼ **teaspoon salt**
	● In a large bowl stir together the 2 cups flour; baking powder; sugar; dried oregano, dried basil, dried savory, or dried marjoram; cream of tartar; and salt.

½ **cup shortening**
½ **cup shredded cheddar,**
     Swiss, or Monterey Jack
     cheese (2 ounces)
	● Use a pastry blender or two knives to cut the shortening into the flour mixture till the mixture resembles coarse crumbs. Stir in cheese. Gently push the mixture against the edges of the bowl, making a well in the center.

⅔ **cup milk** **All-purpose flour**	● Pour the milk into the well. Use a fork to stir just till dough clings together. Knead on a lightly floured surface for 10 to 12 strokes. Pat to ½-inch thickness. Cut with a 2½-inch biscuit cutter, dipping cutter in flour between cuts. Pat scraps together, cut with biscuit cutter. Transfer cut biscuits to an ungreased baking sheet. Bake in a 450° oven for 10 to 12 minutes or till golden. Serve warm. Makes 8 to 10 biscuits.

If these Cheese-Herb Biscuits don't turn out first-rate, it's probably because you undermixed or overmixed the dough. Not mixing or kneading the dough enough will give you biscuits that are small and rough with a spotted crust. The inside will be coarse instead of flaky. If you mix or knead the dough too much, the biscuits will be tough, dry, and have a peak on top.

The best way to avoid these problems is to follow the recipe closely. Be sure to stir the dough just till it clings together. And knead it only 10 to 12 strokes. When you're done, the biscuit dough should be well mixed but not elastic.

Kneading Biscuits

Properly kneading dough mixes the ingredients and helps give structure to biscuits and other breads. Kneading is a technique that you can master with a little practice. Turn the dough out onto a lightly floured surface. Curve your fingers over the dough and use the heel of your hand to pull the dough toward you and then push it away. Rotate the dough a quarter-turn, fold it over, and repeat the process.

Cornmeal Pancakes

TIME: 15 minutes preparation	EQUIPMENT: large bowl liquid measure dry measures griddle measuring spoons pancake turner wooden spoon
1½ cups yellow cornmeal ¼ cup all-purpose flour 1 teaspoon baking soda 1 teaspoon sugar	● In a large bowl stir together the yellow cornmeal, all-purpose flour, baking soda, sugar, and ½ teaspoon *salt*.
1 beaten egg 2 cups buttermilk 2 tablespoons cooking oil	● In a small bowl, stir together the egg, buttermilk, and cooking oil. Add all at once to the dry ingredients, mixing till combined but still slightly lumpy.
Maple-flavored syrup	● Pour about ¼ cup batter for each pancake onto a hot, lightly greased griddle or skillet. Cook till golden brown, turning to cook other side when pancakes have a bubbly surface and slightly dry edges. Serve pancakes with syrup. Makes 16 pancakes.

Cornmeal Pancakes are ready to turn when the tops are bubbly all over, with just a few broken bubbles. The edges of the pancakes will appear slightly dry. Turn your pancakes only once and use a pancake turner or broad spatula.

Pineapple Muffins

TIME: 15 minutes preparation 20 minutes cooking	EQUIPMENT: small bowl dry measures fork measuring spoons can opener muffin pan liquid measure wooden pick wooden spoon wire rack large bowl
1 beaten egg 1 8-ounce can crushed pineapple (juice pack) ⅓ cup cooking oil ¼ cup milk	● Preheat oven to 400°. In a small bowl stir together egg, *undrained* pineapple, cooking oil, and milk. Set aside.
1¾ cups all-purpose flour ¼ cup sugar 2 teaspoons baking powder ¼ teaspoon salt	● In a large bowl stir together flour, sugar, baking powder, and salt. Make a well in the center. Add the egg mixture all at once. Stir just till moistened (batter should be lumpy).
	● Grease 12 muffin cups or line with paper bake cups. Fill each ⅔ full. Bake in a 400° oven for 20 to 25 minutes or till done. Remove from pan to a wire rack. Serve warm. Makes 12 muffins.

Dianna, one of our Test Kitchen home economists, says, "The best muffins are made with minimal mixing. Once you add the egg mixture to the flour mixture, stir just till the ingredients are moistened. Don't try to get all of the lumps out, because a good muffin batter will have a few. If you overmix the batter, the muffins will have a peaked top and tunnels that go toward the peak. A properly mixed muffin will rise evenly and have a slightly rough crust and an open, fairly even texture."

Orange-Wheat Muffins

TIME:	EQUIPMENT:	
15 minutes preparation	small bowl	large bowl
20 minutes cooking	fork	dry measures
	shredder	wooden spoon
	measuring spoons	muffin pan
	liquid measure	wooden pick

Have a few muffins left over? Don't throw them away. Store the leftovers in a covered container at room temperature or wrap them in moisture-vaporproof material and freeze them for up to two months. Frozen muffins should be thawed, unwrapped, at room temperature for one hour, or wrapped in foil and heated in a 300° oven about 25 minutes or till heated through.

1 beaten egg
½ teaspoon finely shredded orange peel
½ cup orange juice
⅓ cup honey
¼ cup cooking oil

● Preheat oven to 375°. In a small bowl stir together the beaten egg, the finely shredded orange peel, orange juice, honey, and cooking oil. Set aside.

1 cup all-purpose flour
½ cup whole wheat flour *or* all-purpose flour
2 teaspoons baking powder
½ teaspoon salt

● In a large bowl stir together the all-purpose flour, whole wheat flour or all-purpose flour, baking powder, and salt. Gently push the flour mixture against the edges of the bowl, making a well in the center. Add the egg mixture all at once, pouring it into the well. Stir just till moistened (batter should be lumpy).

● Grease 10 muffin cups or line with paper bake cups. Fill each ⅔ full. Bake in a 375° oven about 20 minutes or till muffins are done. When done, a wooden pick inserted into the center of a muffin should come out clean. Transfer muffins from pan to a wire rack. Cool slightly. Serve warm. Makes 10 muffins.

Baking Muffins

When you are getting ready to bake your muffin batter, use a muffin pan that has 6 or 12 cuplike indentations. Grease the cups or line them with paper bake cups. Fill the prepared muffin cups only ⅔ full. This allows space for the muffins to rise. An easy way to fill the cups is to scoop up the batter on a spoon and push it off with a rubber scraper. Bake the muffins according to the recipe directions. A perfectly done muffin will have a golden brown top, and when you insert a wooden pick into the center of the muffin, it should come out clean. If you bake the muffins too long they'll be dry and tough. And if you underbake muffins they'll be pale, moist, and heavy.

Blue Ribbon Rolls

TIME:
½ hour preparation
1 hour rising

EQUIPMENT:
small bowl
liquid measure
wooden spoon
small saucepan

dry measures
measuring spoons
rubber spatula

It's county fair time and the competition is on! But don't worry, you're sure to be a winner either at home or at the fair, with Blue Ribbon Rolls. All of the delicious rolls on the next few pages start with this basic yeast roll dough recipe. The next two pages contain detailed step-by-step directions to help you with this recipe. You'll also find pictures and directions to help you shape beautiful rolls, along with baking instructions for every intriguing shape.

1 package active dry yeast ¼ cup warm water (110° to 115°)	● Soften yeast in warm water.
1 cup milk ⅓ cup sugar ⅓ cup butter, margarine, *or* shortening 4 to 4½ cups all-purpose flour 2 eggs	● In a saucepan heat the milk, sugar, butter, and 1 teaspoon *salt* just till warm (115° to 120°) and butter is almost melted. Turn into a large mixing bowl. Stir in *2 cups* of the flour; beat well. Add the softened yeast and eggs; stir till smooth.

● Stir in as much of the remaining flour as you can mix in with a spoon. Turn dough out onto a lightly floured surface. Knead in enough of the remaining flour to make a moderately stiff dough that is smooth and elastic (6 to 8 minutes total). Place in a lightly greased bowl; turn once to grease the surface. Cover; let rise in a warm place till double (about 1 hour).

● Punch down dough; divide it in half. Cover; let rest 10 minutes. Shape and bake desired rolls (see pages 58 and 59).

If your yeast rolls aren't quite up to par, check to see if you have one of these common bread-baking problems—
If the rolls are compact, the rising time was too short, or the liquid used to dissolve the yeast was too hot or too cold.
If the rolls rose nicely, but fell during baking, not enough flour was used or the rolls rose too long and the heat during baking forced the dough to stretch beyond its capacity.

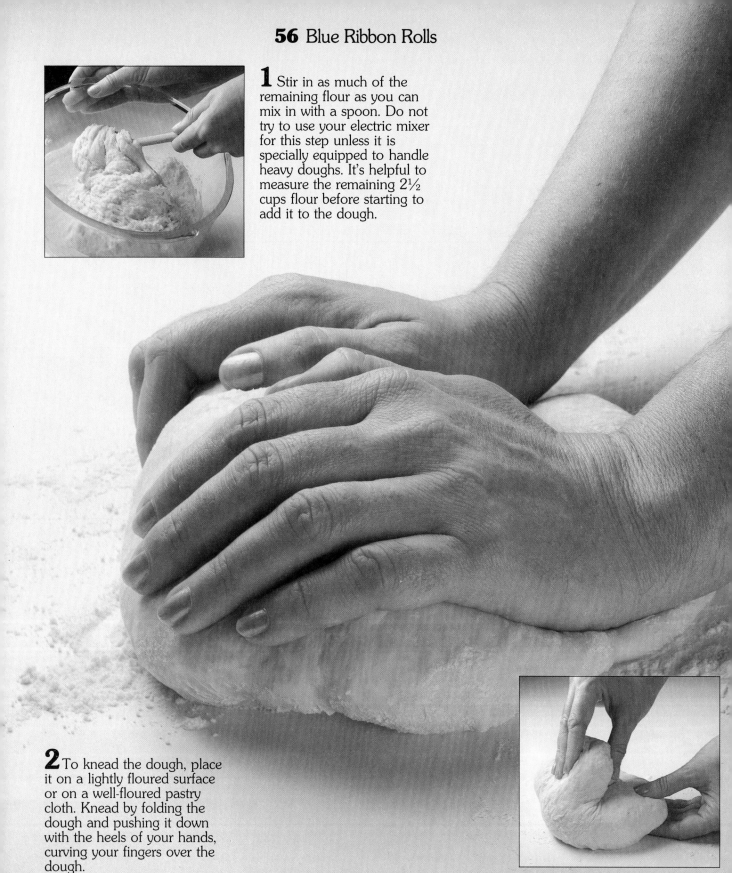

1 Stir in as much of the remaining flour as you can mix in with a spoon. Do not try to use your electric mixer for this step unless it is specially equipped to handle heavy doughs. It's helpful to measure the remaining 2½ cups flour before starting to add it to the dough.

2 To knead the dough, place it on a lightly floured surface or on a well-floured pastry cloth. Knead by folding the dough and pushing it down with the heels of your hands, curving your fingers over the dough.

3 Give the dough a quarter turn, then fold it and push it down again. Continue kneading, adding enough of the remaining flour to prevent stickiness, till the dough is moderately stiff and smooth and elastic.

4 Cover the bowl of dough with a cloth. Set it in the oven (it's a good draft-free place) next to a bowl of hot water. Close the door, but *do not* turn on the oven. Let the dough rise till it is double in size (about 1 hour).

5 You can tell if the dough is doubled and is ready to shape by pressing two fingers ½ inch into the dough. Remove your fingers; if the indentations remain, the dough has doubled in bulk and is ready for the next step.

6 To punch down the yeast roll dough, push your fist into the center of the dough. Pull the edges of the dough to the center. Then turn the dough over and place it on a lightly floured surface.

7 Cut the dough in half. Shape each half into a smooth ball. Place the balls on a lightly floured surface. Cover with a towel. Let stand (rest) for 10 minutes; this makes the dough easier to shape.

Filled Rolls

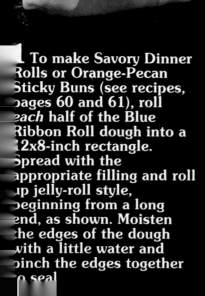

2 Slice *each* roll into 12 pieces. Place ordinary sewing-weight thread under the dough where you want to make the cut. Pull the thread up and around sides. Crisscross the thread across the top, pulling quickly as though tying a knot.

1 To make Savory Dinner Rolls or Orange-Pecan Sticky Buns (see recipes, pages 60 and 61), roll *each* half of the Blue Ribbon Roll dough into a 12x8-inch rectangle. Spread with the appropriate filling and roll up jelly-roll style, beginning from a long end, as shown. Moisten the edges of the dough with a little water and pinch the edges together to seal.

3 Arrange the slices in the pan you have prepared according to the recipes on pages 60 or 61. Let the rolls rise, and bake according to the recipes.

Cloverleaf Rolls

Cloverleaf rolls are one of the easiest shapes to make. Start by lightly greasing 24 muffin cups. Divide the Blue Ribbon Roll dough (see recipe, page 54) into 72 equal-size pieces. Shape each piece into a ball, pulling edges under to make a smooth top. Place 3 balls in each muffin cup, smooth side up. Cover; let rise till nearly double (about 30 minutes). Bake in a 375° oven for 12 to 15 minutes or till done. Makes 24 rolls.

Butterhorns

For butterhorns, on a lightly floured surface roll *each* half of Blue Ribbon Roll dough (see recipe, page 54) into a 12-inch circle. Brush with some melted *butter*. Cut *each* circle into 12 wedges. Beginning at the wide end of *each* wedge, roll toward the point. Place rolls point side down, 2 to 3 inches apart on greased baking sheets. Cover; let rise in a warm place till nearly double (about 30 minutes). Bake in a 375° oven for 12 to 15 minutes. Makes 24 rolls.

Rosettes

1 You don't have to be a Boy Scout to tie the knots for rosettes. Just divide Blue Ribbon Roll dough (see recipe, page 54) into 32 equal-size pieces. On a floured surface, roll each piece into a 12-inch rope.

2 Tie each rope into a loose knot leaving two long ends, as shown above. Tuck the top end under the roll. Bring bottom end up and tuck it into the center of roll.

3 Place 2 to 3 inches apart on a greased baking sheet. Cover; let rise till nearly double (about 30 minutes). Bake in a 375° oven for 12 to 15 minutes or till done. Makes 32.

Orange-Pecan Sticky Buns

TIME:
1 hour preparation
1½ hours rising
20 minutes cooking

EQUIPMENT:
rolling pin
small bowl
dry measures
shredder
measuring spoons
wooden spoon
small saucepan
pastry brush
two 9x1½-inch
  round baking
  pans
thread
serving plates

To get a slightly different flavor, substitute almost any other nut (chopped walnuts, peanut halves, slivered almonds, chopped black walnuts, or chopped macadamia nuts) for the chopped pecans.

Blue Ribbon Roll dough
(see recipe, page 54)
½ cup packed brown sugar
1 teaspoon finely shredded orange peel
¼ cup butter *or* margarine, melted

● Prepare roll dough as directed on page 54. On a lightly floured surface roll *half* of the dough into a 12x8-inch rectangle. In a small bowl stir together ½ cup brown sugar and 1 teaspoon orange peel. Use a pastry brush to brush *half* of ¼ cup melted butter or margarine over the rolled out dough. Sprinkle with *half* of the brown sugar mixture. Roll up jelly-roll style, beginning at a long side. Moisten edges of dough with water. Pinch together to seal firmly. Repeat with remaining dough, melted butter or margarine, and brown sugar mixture.

⅔ cup packed brown sugar
¼ cup butter *or* margarine
2 tablespoons light corn syrup
1 teaspoon finely shredded orange peel
½ cup chopped pecans

● In a small saucepan stir together the ⅔ cup brown sugar, ¼ cup butter or margarine, light corn syrup, and 1 teaspoon finely shredded orange peel. Cook and stir over medium heat till combined. Pour *half* of the mixture into *each* of two ungreased 9x1½-inch round baking pans. Sprinkle *each* pan with ¼ *cup* of the pecans.

● Cut each roll of dough into 12 slices. Instead of using a sharp knife, use a piece of ordinary sewing-weight or heavy-duty thread. Place the thread under the roll of dough where you want to make the cut. Pull thread up around the sides of the dough. Crisscross thread across the top of the roll, pulling quickly as though tying a knot.

● Place *12* rolls atop the brown sugar mixture in *each* pan. Cover; let rise till nearly double (about 30 minutes). Bake in a 375° oven for 20 to 25 minutes or till rolls are done. Invert onto serving plates. Makes 24 rolls.

Freezing Rolls

Because the recipes for Orange-Pecan Sticky Buns and Savory Dinner Rolls make two pans of buns, you may want to store one pan for later use. If so, wrap the buns in moisture-vaporproof paper, label, and freeze them. Then, when you want to use the buns, just thaw them at room temperature and heat them in a warm oven for a few minutes or till they are warm through.

Savory Dinner Rolls

TIME:
45 minutes preparation
1½ hours rising
15 minutes cooking

EQUIPMENT:
two 9x1½-inch
   round baking
   pans
small saucepan
knife
dry measures

measuring spoons
wooden spoon
rolling pin
thread
serving plates

To get the dough rolled out to the right shape, place half of the dough on a lightly floured surface. Use a rolling pin and roll from the center to the edges with light, even strokes, forming a 12x8-inch rectangle. You can reshape the dough into a rectangle with your hands as you work.

Blue Ribbon Roll dough (see recipe, page 54)

● Grease two 9x1½-inch round baking pans. Set aside. Prepare roll dough as directed on page 54.

⅓ cup sliced green onion
3 tablespoons sesame seed
¼ cup butter *or* margarine
3 tablespoons grated
   Parmesan cheese

● In a small saucepan cook the sliced green onion and sesame seed in the butter or margarine till the green onion is tender. Stir in the Parmesan cheese.

● On a lightly floured surface roll out *half* of the roll dough into a 12x8-inch rectangle. Spread *half* of the onion mixture over the dough. Roll up jelly-roll style, beginning at a long side. Moisten edges of dough with water. Pinch together to seal firmly. Repeat with remaining dough and onion mixture.

● Slice each roll of dough into 12 pieces. Instead of using a sharp knife, use a piece of ordinary sewing-weight or heavy-duty thread. Place the thread under the roll of dough where you want to make the cut. Pull the thread up around the sides of the dough. Crisscross thread across top of roll, pulling quickly as though tying a knot.

Savory Dinner Rolls are a delicious complement to pot roast. The onion flavor of the rolls goes well with the milder flavor of the roasted meat.

● Place *12* rolls in *each* of the prepared pans. Cover; let rise till nearly double (about 30 minutes). Bake in a 375° oven for 15 to 18 minutes or till rolls are done. Cool in pans for 10 minutes. Remove to serving plates. Serve warm. Makes 24 rolls.

Tailgate Party

Two bits, four bits, six bits, a dollar! All for a tailgate party, stand up and holler! Tailgate parties and the "big game" go together to create memories of good friends, fun, exciting games, and wonderful food. For your next tailgate party, prepare this easy menu (see recipes, pages 64-67). Your friends are sure to love the out-of-the-ordinary foods.

MENU

Italian Sausages in Brioche
Tailgate Coleslaw *or*
    Italian-Style Pasta Salad
Fresh fruit
Soft drinks or beer

Italian Sausages in Brioche

Pictured on pages 62-63—

TIME:
30 minutes preparation
2½ hours rising
45 minutes cooking
2 hours refrigeration

EQUIPMENT:

small bowl	rubber spatula
liquid measure	plastic wrap
small saucepan	knife
dry measures	wire rack
measuring spoons	baking pan
wooden spoon	paper toweling

---

1 **package active dry yeast** ⅓ **cup warm water (110° to 115°)** ⅓ **cup milk** ⅓ **cup butter *or* margarine** ¼ **cup sugar** ¼ **teaspoon salt** 3 **cups all-purpose flour** 2 **eggs, beaten**	● Soften yeast in warm water. In a saucepan heat milk, butter or margarine, sugar, and salt till warm (115° to 120°) and butter is almost melted; stir constantly. Turn into a large mixing bowl. Stir in *1 cup* of the flour; beat well. Add the softened yeast and eggs; stir till smooth. Stir in the remaining flour.

	● Scrape down sides of bowl, forming dough into ball. Cover bowl with plastic wrap. Refrigerate for 2 to 24 hours.

---

8 **links Italian sausage (about 2 pounds)**	● Meanwhile, split Italian sausage links lengthwise. Place cut side down, on a rack in a shallow baking pan. Bake, uncovered, in a 350° oven for 25 to 30 minutes or till done. Drain sausages on paper toweling. Let cool about 30 minutes or till nearly room temperature.

---

3 **tablespoons prepared mustard** 2 **slices cheddar, mozzarella, *or* Swiss cheese**	● Spread cut sides of sausages with mustard. Cut cheese into eight 5x¾-inch strips. Place 1 strip on cut side of *8* sausage halves. Top with remaining sausage halves, forming 8 stacks.

---

1 **egg white** 1 **tablespoon water**	● Remove dough from refrigerator. Punch down. Transfer to a lightly floured surface. Divide into 8 equal portions. With floured hands or rolling pin, flatten each into an 8x5-inch oval. Place 1 sausage link on each oval. Wrap dough around sausages, pressing edges to seal. Place seam side down on a greased shallow baking pan. Stir together egg white and water. Brush some egg white mixture atop each. Cover and let rise till nearly double (about 30 to 40 minutes).

	● Bake in a 375° oven for 15 to 18 minutes or till golden. Remove to a wire rack to cool. Wrap tightly and refrigerate. Makes 8 main-dish servings.

MENU COUNTDOWN
1 Day Ahead:
Prepare Italian Sausages in Brioche and refrigerate.
Prepare Tailgate Coleslaw *or* Italian-Style Pasta Salad and refrigerate.
Chill pop or beer.
Pack all nonfood items.
Day of Party:
Pack Italian Sausages in Brioche, Tailgate Coleslaw, *or* Italian-Style Pasta Salad, and pop or beer in cooler.
Pack fresh fruit.

To get rid of excess fat, place the split Italian sausage links, cut side down on a rack in a shallow baking pan.

Place the two halves of the cut Italian sausage links back together, forming a link.

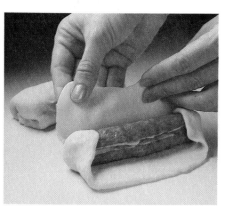

Wrap the brioche dough around the Italian sausage links, pressing the edges of the dough to seal.

Planning a Tailgate Party

It doesn't take hard work, just a little careful planning, to assemble a tailgate party (like the one shown on pages 62 and 63). Start by deciding what nonfood essentials you'll need and pack those first.

Because you won't be using picnic tables in the stadium parking lot, you'll want to pack lawn chairs, a blanket, or plastic ground cloth to sit on. You'll also need a tablecloth, napkins, plastic or paper plates and cups, plastic or regular flatware, moist towelettes, serving utensils, and plastic or paper garbage bags. Pack for convenience and safety. For example, wrap each flatware setting in a napkin to keep it from rattling in your picnic basket and to speed up "table" setting. Or, use the ground cloth or tablecloth as a wrapper to protect any glass containers.

Avoid taking creamed foods such as custards, puddings, and cream pies because they are susceptible to bacterial growth. Pack the foods for the tailgate party last thing before leaving home. Have everything tightly wrapped. Make sure cold foods are well chilled in advance and kept cold in a cooler. Also, be sure to keep warm foods warm.

Tailgate Coleslaw

Pictured on pages 62-63

TIME:	EQUIPMENT:	
25 minutes advance preparation	large bowl shredder dry measures vegetable peeler knife	measuring spoons fork screw-top jar liquid measure

Use the side of the shredder with large holes to shred the cabbage for Tailgate Coleslaw.

3 cups shredded cabbage **1 cup shredded carrot** **½ cup sliced cucumber** **2 tablespoons sliced green onion**	● In a large bowl toss together the shredded cabbage, shredded carrot, sliced cucumber, and sliced green onion.
¼ cup vinegar **2 tablespoons brown sugar** **1 tablespoon salad oil** **½ teaspoon dry mustard** **½ teaspoon salt**	● In a screw-top jar combine vinegar, brown sugar, salad oil, dry mustard, and salt. Cover and shake well. Pour over combined vegetables. Toss to coat vegetables. Cover and refrigerate for 3 to 24 hours. Toss before serving. Makes 8 side-dish servings.

Italian-Style Pasta Salad

TIME:
30 minutes advance preparation

EQUIPMENT:

large saucepan
liquid measure
measuring spoons
colander
knife
large bowl

shredder
screw-top jar
garlic press
fork

1½ **quarts water**
¼ **teaspoon salt**
4 **ounces spaghetti**

● In a large saucepan bring water and salt to a rolling boil. Break the spaghetti in half. Add the spaghetti to the boiling water a little at a time so water does not stop boiling. Reduce heat slightly and continue boiling, uncovered, for 10 to 12 minutes or till the spaghetti is tender, but still slightly firm. Stir occasionally. Drain the spaghetti in a colander. Set aside.

1 **6-ounce jar marinated artichoke hearts**
½ **of a small zucchini**

● In a colander drain artichokes, reserving marinade. Coarsely chop artichokes. Lengthwise halve the zucchini. Slice each half.

1 **cup shredded mozzarella cheese (4 ounces)**
1 **medium carrot, shredded**
2 **ounces sliced salami, cut into strips**
2 **tablespoons grated Parmesan cheese**

● In a large bowl combine the cooked spaghetti, chopped artichoke hearts, sliced zucchini, shredded mozzarella cheese, shredded carrot, salami strips, and grated Parmesan cheese.

2 **tablespoons salad oil**
2 **tablespoons white wine vinegar**
¾ **teaspoon dry mustard**
½ **teaspoon dried oregano, crushed**
½ **teaspoon dried basil, crushed**
1 **clove garlic, minced**

● In a screw-top jar combine the reserved artichoke marinade, salad oil, white wine vinegar, dry mustard, dried oregano, dried basil, and minced garlic. Cover tightly and shake well. Pour over spaghetti mixture; toss to coat evenly. Cover and chill for several hours or overnight. Toss before serving. Makes 8 side-dish servings.

Substitute Italian-Style Pasta Salad for the Tailgate Coleslaw at your next Tailgate Party. Legend has it that Marco Polo took pasta home to Italy from the Orient in the thirteenth century. However, some Italians argue vehemently that pasta was eaten in Rome well before Polo ever set out on his journey. The first pasta seen in the United States was introduced by Thomas Jefferson in 1786, when he brought from Italy an early version of a pasta machine. It wasn't until much later, however, that pasta gained its popularity.

Salad Ingredients

Greens	Cauliflower
Mushrooms	Zucchini
Radishes	Broccoli
Carrots	Avocados
Tomatoes	Fruits
Cucumbers	Celery
Onions	Croutons
Green	Seeds
peppers	Olives
Parsley	Sprouts
Fresh herbs	Water
Cheeses	chestnuts
Nuts	Meats

You don't have to be a rabbit or dieting to love a tossed salad. With the infinite number of salad ingredients available year round, you can create a salad to suit almost anyone's taste. On these two pages we've suggested possible ingredients. Put them together and improvise the salad of your choice.

Yes, you do wash greens (any of the various lettuces—endive, leaf, escarole, romaine, watercress, Bibb, iceberg, or Boston and spinach) before you put them into a salad. But forget the soap—cool water will do the job. Also remove roots, damaged portions, and large veins, if present. Pat dry with paper toweling, and tear into bite-size pieces.

Sprouts, most commonly mung and alfalfa, are a delicious addition to salads. Sprouts are nothing more than untreated seeds that have just begun to grow, but they add a tang to a salad.

Fresh mushrooms are a delicious addition to a salad. But before you use mushrooms, gently rinse them in cold water and pat them dry. If you want to slice the mushrooms, slice right through the caps and stems.

Don't forget, fresh or canned fruits are a flavorful addition to a salad. Try orange or grapefruit sections, chunks of apple or pineapple, or peach or pear slices.

Radishes add color as well as zip to any salad. Wash radishes in cool water and trim off the leaves and root ends before thinly slicing them.

Wash and trim carrots before using them in a salad. Scrub carrots with a stiff brush or wash and peel them. Then, slice or shred the carrots.

Wash tomatoes and cherry tomatoes before you use them. You can leave cherry tomatoes whole for a salad, but cut large tomatoes into wedges.

Shrimp and Grapefruit Salad

TIME: **20 minutes preparation** **30 minutes chilling**	EQUIPMENT: knife liquid measure small bowl fork large bowl pastry brush dry measures salad plates
1 medium grapefruit	● Use a sharp knife to cut the peel and white membrane off the grapefruit. Working over a small bowl, remove the sections by cutting into the center of the fruit between one section and the membrane. Then turn the knife and slide it down the other side of the section next to the membrane. Remove any seeds. Repeat with remaining sections. Cut each section into 1-inch pieces. Reserve juice in the bowl.
1 6-ounce package frozen cooked shrimp, thawed **½ cup thinly sliced cucumber** **¼ cup sweet white wine**	● In a large bowl toss together the grapefruit, shrimp, cucumber, and wine. Cover and chill for 30 minutes to 1 hour.
½ medium avocado	● Peel the avocado and cut it into ½-inch pieces. Brush the avocado pieces with the reserved grapefruit juice. Toss the avocado with the grapefruit mixture.
Lettuce leaves	● Line two salad plates with lettuce leaves. Spoon the grapefruit mixture atop. Makes 2 main-dish servings.

Avocados have been enjoyed by the peoples of the tropical sections of the Americas for years. The Mayas of Mexico were enjoying the fruit as early as 300 B.C. The ancient Aztecs called avocados ahuacatl. And later, George Washington sampled them on a trip to the Barbados in 1751.

Tangy Herbed Salad Dressing

TIME:
10 minutes preparation
1 hour chilling

EQUIPMENT:

small bowl	knife
dry measures	garlic press
measuring spoons	wooden spoon

Surprise your family and friends with homemade salad dressing. Tangy Herbed Salad Dressing is easy to make and the herbed flavor is so much better than bottled dressing. If you have some dressing left over, store it in a tightly covered container in the refrigerator for up to 1 week.

1 cup mayonnaise *or* salad dressing
2 tablespoons lemon *or* lime juice
1 tablespoon sliced green onion
1 tablespoon milk
1 teaspoon Worcestershire sauce
½ teaspoon dried basil, oregano, thyme, *or* marjoram, crushed
1 clove garlic, minced, *or* ⅛ teaspoon garlic powder

● In a small bowl stir together mayonnaise or salad dressing; lemon or lime juice; sliced green onion; milk; Worcestershire sauce; dried crushed basil, oregano, thyme, or marjoram; and garlic. Cover and chill at least 1 hour.

Torn salad greens

● Serve atop torn salad greens. Makes about 1¼ cups dressing.

Creamy Fruit Dressing

TIME:
10 minutes preparation

EQUIPMENT:

small bowl	shredder
dry measures	wooden spoon
measuring spoons	spoon

Poppy seeds are tiny, slate-blue seeds that are so small it takes about 900,000 to make a pound. Although poppy seeds appear to be round, they're actually kidney-shaped, and most are imported from Holland.

½ cup mayonnaise *or* salad dressing
½ cup dairy sour cream
1 tablespoon honey
1 teaspoon poppy seed
½ teaspoon finely shredded orange peel

● In a small bowl stir together the mayonnaise or salad dressing, dairy sour cream, honey, poppy seed, and finely shredded orange peel.

2 to 3 tablespoons orange juice *or* milk
Desired fresh fruits, cut up

● Stir in enough orange juice or milk to make the dressing of desired consistency. Spoon over desired cut-up fresh fruit. Makes 1¼ cups dressing.

Cheese Sauce

TIME:	EQUIPMENT:	
5 minutes preparation	small saucepan	dry measures
10 minutes cooking	measuring spoons	liquid measure
	wooden spoon	shredder

1 tablespoon butter *or* margarine 1 tablespoon all-purpose flour	● In a small saucepan melt the butter or margarine. Stir in the all-purpose flour and a dash *pepper.*
⅔ cup milk	● Add the milk all at once. Cook and stir over medium heat till the mixture is thickened and bubbly. Cook and stir 1 minute more.
½ cup shredded cheddar, Swiss, American, Edam, Gruyère, Monterey Jack, Fontina, *or* Gouda cheese Steamed vegetables	● Over low heat stir in cheddar, Swiss, American, Edam, Gruyère, Monterey Jack, Fontina, or Gouda cheese till melted. Serve over steamed vegetables (see recipes below and at right). Makes 1½ cups sauce.

In a heavy saucepan melt the butter or margarine over low heat. Stir in the flour and pepper with a wooden spoon till no lumps remain.

Steamed Cauliflower

TIME:	EQUIPMENT:	
10 minutes preparation	knife	large saucepan
12 minutes cooking	steamer basket	

½ head cauliflower	● Wash cauliflower. Remove leaves and woody stem. Break into flowerets. Place flowerets in a steamer basket. Place basket in a large saucepan over, but not touching, boiling water. Cover; reduce heat. Steam for 12 to 15 minutes or just till tender. Makes 4 side-dish servings.

With the saucepan over low heat, add the milk all at once. Stir constantly to evenly distribute the fat-flour mixture, so the sauce will not be lumpy.

Steamer Baskets

If you don't have a steamer basket, you can make a substitute. Invert a small heat-proof bowl in the bottom of a Dutch oven. Pour water around the bowl. Then, punch several holes in the bottom of an aluminum foil pie plate. Place your vegetables in the pie plate. Bring the water to boiling and set the pie plate on the bottom of the bowl. Steam your vegetables according to recipe directions.

After the milk mixture is thickened and bubbly, add the cheese to the sauce. Stir constantly till the cheese is melted.

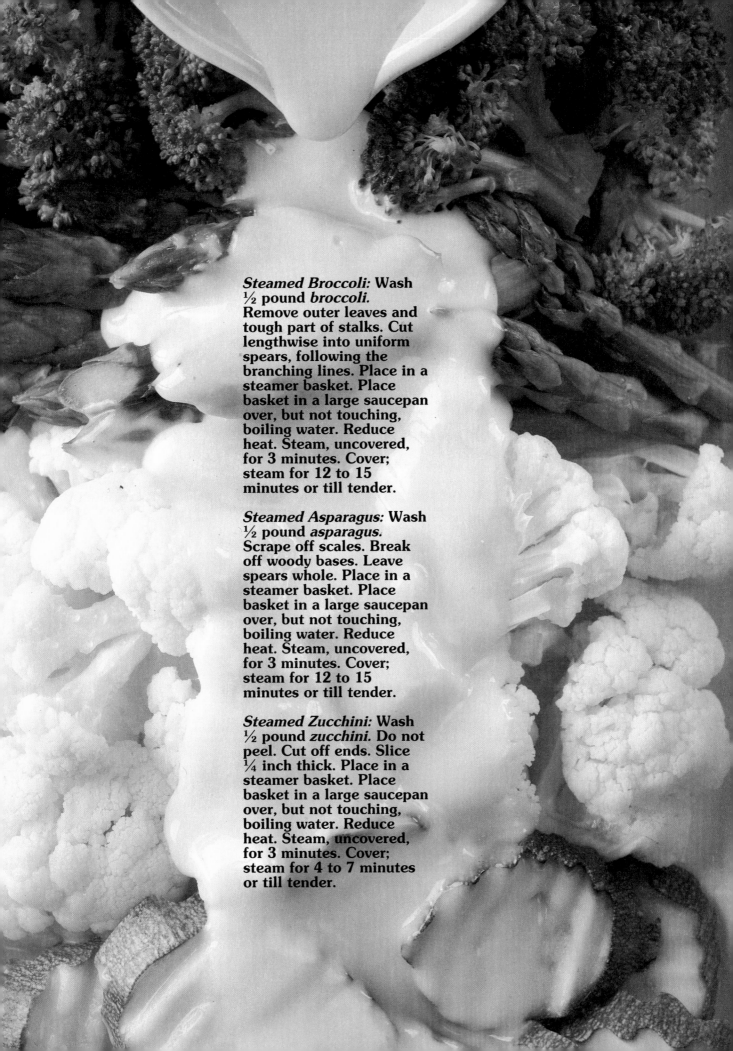

Steamed Broccoli: Wash ½ pound *broccoli.* Remove outer leaves and tough part of stalks. Cut lengthwise into uniform spears, following the branching lines. Place in a steamer basket. Place basket in a large saucepan over, but not touching, boiling water. Reduce heat. Steam, uncovered, for 3 minutes. Cover; steam for 12 to 15 minutes or till tender.

Steamed Asparagus: Wash ½ pound *asparagus.* Scrape off scales. Break off woody bases. Leave spears whole. Place in a steamer basket. Place basket in a large saucepan over, but not touching, boiling water. Reduce heat. Steam, uncovered, for 3 minutes. Cover; steam for 12 to 15 minutes or till tender.

Steamed Zucchini: Wash ½ pound *zucchini.* Do not peel. Cut off ends. Slice ¼ inch thick. Place in a steamer basket. Place basket in a large saucepan over, but not touching, boiling water. Reduce heat. Steam, uncovered, for 3 minutes. Cover; steam for 4 to 7 minutes or till tender.

Cream of Tomato Soup

TIME:	EQUIPMENT:	
10 minutes preparation	saucepan	measuring spoons
20 minutes cooking	can opener	wooden spoon
	liquid measure	blender
	knife	spatula

After you feel confident making this tomato soup, branch out into one of the other variations—Cream of Celery Soup, Cream of Broccoli Soup, or Cream of Mushroom Soup. It won't be long before you're a pro at making homemade soups!

1 7½-ounce can tomatoes, cut up
¾ cup water
2 tablespoons chopped onion
1 teaspoon instant chicken bouillon granules
⅛ teaspoon dried basil, crushed

● In a saucepan stir together the *undrained* tomatoes, water, chopped onion, chicken bouillon granules, and crushed dried basil. Bring mixture to boiling.
Reduce heat; cover and simmer vegetable mixture for 10 minutes.

● Place the vegetable mixture in a blender container or food processor bowl. Cover and process for 30 seconds to 1 minute or till mixture is smooth.

1 tablespoon butter *or* margarine
1 tablespoon all-purpose flour
Dash pepper
½ cup milk

● In the same saucepan melt the butter or margarine. Stir in the flour and pepper. Add the milk all at once. Cook and stir over medium heat till the mixture is thickened and bubbly. Cook and stir 1 minute more. Gradually stir in the hot blended vegetable mixture. Cook and stir till heated through. Makes 2 side-dish servings.

Cream of Celery Soup

By making only a few changes to the recipe for Cream of Tomato Soup, you can prepare deliciously seasoned Cream of Celery Soup, Cream of Mushroom Soup, or Cream of Broccoli Soup.

• Prepare Cream of Tomato Soup as directed, *except* substitute ¾ cup chopped *celery* for the tomatoes and add 1 teaspoon snipped *parsley* along with the basil. Continue as directed.

Cream of Broccoli Soup

• Cream of Broccoli Soup makes an elegant appetizer as well as a delicious side dish. The recipe makes two side-dish servings or four appetizer servings.
• Prepare Cream of Tomato Soup as directed, *except* substitute 1 cup cut fresh *broccoli* or frozen *broccoli,* thawed, for the tomatoes, and substitute ¼ teaspoon crushed dried *marjoram* or crushed dried *thyme* for the basil. Stir in a dash of *garlic powder.* Continue as directed in the recipe.

Cream of Mushroom Soup

• One of our editors said this Cream of Mushroom Soup is the best she's ever tasted. Why don't you give it a try and see what you think.
• Prepare Cream of Tomato Soup as directed, *except* substitute ½ cup sliced fresh *mushrooms* for the tomatoes and substitute 1 teaspoon snipped *parsley* for the basil. Stir in ¼ teaspoon crushed dried *marjoram.* Bring the mixture to boiling. Reduce heat; cover and simmer for 5 minutes instead of 10 minutes. Continue as directed.

Twice-Baked Cheesy Potatoes

TIME: 1½ hours total preparation	EQUIPMENT:	
	vegetable brush	potato masher
	fork	measuring spoons
	knife	dry measures
	spoon	shredder
	bowl	baking pan

4 medium potatoes **Shortening**	● Scrub baking potatoes with a brush. For soft skins, rub with shortening. Prick potatoes with a fork. Bake in a 425° oven for 40 to 60 minutes or till tender.
	● Use a knife to cut a lengthwise slice from the top of each potato; discard skin from slice. Use a spoon to scoop out the inside of each potato, leaving a ½-inch shell. Set potato shells aside.
2 tablespoons butter *or* margarine **½ cup dairy sour cream** **⅛ teaspoon pepper** **½ cup shredded American cheese (2 ounces)** **¼ cup cooked bacon pieces (optional)**	● In a bowl mash the slices from tops of potatoes and the insides of potatoes. Add butter or margarine. Beat in sour cream and pepper. Stir in the shredded American cheese and cooked bacon pieces, if desired.
	● Spoon or pipe the potato mixture into the potato shells. Place in a shallow baking pan. Bake in a 425° oven for 20 to 25 minutes or till lightly browned. Makes 4 side-dish servings.

If you don't have American cheese on hand, try substituting cheddar, Swiss, Monterey Jack, mozzarella, or pepper cheese. You also can substitute two slices of bacon that have been cooked, drained, and crumbled for the cooked bacon bits.

Orange-Buttered Carrots

TIME:	EQUIPMENT:	
8 minutes preparation	small saucepan	measuring spoons
10 minutes cooking	knife	shredder
	colander	fork
	serving bowl	

To bias-slice the carrots for this recipe, hold the knife at a 45-degree angle and cut across the carrots, making slices that are ¼ inch thick.

6 medium carrots, bias-sliced ¼ inch thick	● In a small saucepan cook carrots, covered, in 1 inch of boiling salted water for 10 to 15 minutes or just till tender. Drain and transfer to a serving bowl.
2 tablespoons butter *or* margarine ½ teaspoon finely shredded orange peel 1 tablespoon orange juice	● Immediately toss carrots with butter or margarine, shredded orange peel, and orange juice. Makes 4 side-dish servings.

Buying and Storing Carrots

Although fresh carrots are most abundant from January to June, you'll find them at your supermarket year round. When you buy carrots, make sure they're firm, well shaped, smooth, clean, and bright golden-orange in color. Large chubby carrots with cracks are likely to be overgrown and tough. If you buy carrots with tops, make sure the leaves are fresh and bright green. Once you have the carrots at home, remove any tops and place the unwashed carrots in a plastic bag. Store them in the crisper compartment of your refrigerator for up to four weeks.

Chocolate Chip Cookies

TIME:	EQUIPMENT:	
20 minutes preparation	medium bowl	rubber spatula
	dry measures	teaspoon
	measuring spoons	cookie sheet
	wooden spoon	pancake turner
	mixer bowl	wire rack
	electric mixer	

2½ cups all-purpose flour 1 teaspoon baking soda	● In a medium bowl stir together flour and baking soda. Set aside.
1 cup butter *or* margarine 1 cup packed brown sugar ½ cup sugar	● In a large mixer bowl beat butter or margarine on medium speed of an electric mixer for 30 seconds. Add brown sugar and sugar; beat till fluffy.
2 eggs 1½ teaspoons vanilla	● Add eggs and vanilla; beat well. Add dry ingredients to the mixture, beating till well combined.
1 12-ounce package (2 cups) semisweet chocolate pieces	● Stir in chocolate pieces. Drop dough from a teaspoon 2 inches apart onto an ungreased cookie sheet. Bake in a 375° oven for 8 to 10 minutes or till done (see tip at right). Remove from oven. Cool on cookie sheet for 1 minute. Use a pancake turner to move cookies to a wire rack to completely cool. Makes about 60 cookies.

You can test the cookies for doneness by gently touching a lightly browned cookie with your fingertip. The imprint should be barely visible. If the cookies are not yet done, the imprint of your fingertip will be large and the cookies will be doughy. If the cookies are overbaked, you will not be able to see any imprint and the cookies will be dry and hard.

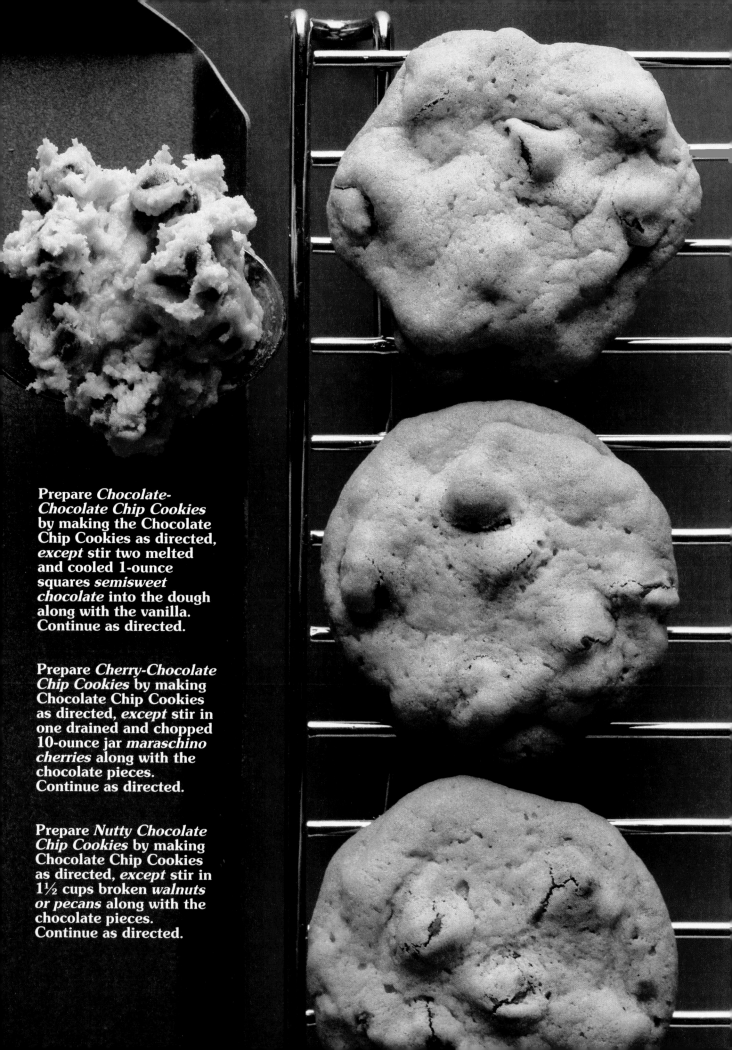

Prepare *Chocolate-Chocolate Chip Cookies* by making the Chocolate Chip Cookies as directed, *except* stir two melted and cooled 1-ounce squares *semisweet chocolate* into the dough along with the vanilla. Continue as directed.

Prepare *Cherry-Chocolate Chip Cookies* by making Chocolate Chip Cookies as directed, *except* stir in one drained and chopped 10-ounce jar *maraschino cherries* along with the chocolate pieces. Continue as directed.

Prepare *Nutty Chocolate Chip Cookies* by making Chocolate Chip Cookies as directed, *except* stir in 1½ cups broken *walnuts or pecans* along with the chocolate pieces. Continue as directed.

Yellow Birthday Cake

TIME:	EQUIPMENT:	
25 minutes preparation	round baking pans	mixer bowl
25 to 30 minutes cooking	medium bowl	electric mixer
	dry measures	rubber spatula
	measuring spoons	liquid measure
	wooden spoon	wire rack

To add decorative touches to the frosted cake, buy an aerosol can or squeeze tube of decorator's frosting. Try practicing with the decorator's frosting on waxed paper. Once you've found a design that you like, add it to the cake.

2¾ cups all-purpose flour
2½ teaspoons baking powder
½ teaspoon salt

● Grease and lightly flour two 8x1½-inch or two 9x1½-inch round baking pans. In a medium bowl stir together flour, baking powder, and salt.

½ cup butter *or* margarine
1¾ cups sugar
1½ teaspoons vanilla
2 eggs

● In a large mixer bowl beat butter on medium speed for 30 seconds. Add sugar and vanilla; beat till well combined. Add eggs, one at a time, beating well on medium speed.

1¼ cups milk

● Add dry ingredients and milk alternately to mixture, beating after each addition. Turn into pans. Bake in a 375° oven till a wooden pick inserted near center comes out clean. (Allow 30 to 35 minutes for 8-inch cakes and 25 to 30 minutes for 9-inch cakes.) Cool in pans for 10 minutes on wire racks. Invert pans on wire racks to remove cakes. Cool completely. Frost and decorate as desired (see tips, below and right). Makes 12 dessert servings.

Frosting Cakes

Assemble the cake by placing one baked layer, top side down, on a serving plate. Tuck several strips of waxed paper under the edge of the cake. Use a metal spatula to spread about ½ cup of frosting (canned or mix frosting will work fine) over this layer. Place the remaining baked layer, top side up, over the frosted layer. Make sure the edges of the cake layers align. Now you're ready for the second step—frosting the outside of the cake. Starting with the sides, spread the frosting on the cake, smoothing the frosting with the edge of a metal spatula held upright against the side of the cake. Then spread the top of the cake with frosting to meet the frosting on the sides, keeping the spatula almost parallel to the top surface of the cake. Smooth all the frosting with the edge of the metal spatula. Remove the waxed paper.

Chocolate Chip Birthday Cake: Prepare the Yellow Birthday Cake as directed, *except* after adding dry ingredients and milk, fold in ½ cup *mini semisweet chocolate pieces.*

Nutmeg Birthday Cake: Prepare the Yellow Birthday Cake as directed, *except* stir 2 teaspoons *ground nutmeg* into the flour mixture.

Citrus Birthday Cake: Prepare Yellow Birthday Cake as directed, *except* stir 1 tablespoon *finely shredded orange peel* and 1½ teaspoons *finely shredded lemon peel* into the flour mixture.

Apple-Orange Bars

TIME:	EQUIPMENT:	
15 minutes preparation	12x7½x2-inch	measuring spoons
25 minutes cooking	baking pan	large bowl
	medium saucepan	wooden pick
	dry measures	knife
	wooden spoon	wire rack
	fork	medium bowl
	shredder	sifter

1 cup packed brown sugar ⅓ cup butter *or* margarine	● Grease a 12x7½x2-inch baking pan. In a medium saucepan combine the brown sugar and the butter or margarine. Cook and stir the mixture over medium heat till the butter is melted.
1 beaten egg ½ cup applesauce 1 teaspoon finely shredded orange peel 1 teaspoon vanilla	● Stir the beaten egg, applesauce, finely shredded orange peel, and vanilla into the butter-sugar mixture in the saucepan.
1¼ cups all-purpose flour 1 teaspoon baking powder ½ teaspoon salt ¼ teaspoon baking soda ½ cup chopped pecans	● In a large bowl stir together the flour, baking powder, salt, and baking soda. Stir the applesauce mixture and chopped pecans into the flour mixture. Spread in prepared baking pan.
Orange Glaze	● Bake in a 350° oven about 25 minutes or till cookies are done. Cool 10 minutes on wire rack. While warm, spread with Orange Glaze. Cool completely. Cut into bars. Makes 18 bars.
	● **Orange Glaze:** In a medium mixing bowl stir together 1½ cups sifted *powdered sugar,* 2 tablespoons *orange juice,* and ½ teaspoon *vanilla* till the mixture is smooth.

Maryellyn, one of our Test Kitchen home economists, says, "I always test bar cookies for doneness by inserting a wooden pick into the center of the baked cookies. If the pick comes out clean, I know they are done. However, if the pick comes out with some batter still on it, I allow the cookies to bake a minute or two longer or till they test done with a wooden pick."

Another time, try substituting finely shredded lemon peel for the orange peel in the bars and lemon juice for the orange juice in the glaze.

Chocolate Syrup Brownies

TIME:	EQUIPMENT:	
15 minutes preparation	13x9x2-inch baking	can opener
30 minutes cooking	pan	wooden spoon
	mixer bowl	wire rack
	rubber spatula	small saucepan
	electric mixer	measuring spoons
	dry measures	

Chocolate Syrup Brownies is a favorite recipe of several of our food editors because it not only makes a rich moist brownie, it also is a quick dessert to prepare after work.

½ cup butter *or* margarine
1 cup sugar
4 eggs

● Grease a 13x9x2-inch baking pan. In a large mixer bowl beat butter or margarine on medium speed of an electric mixer for 30 seconds. Add sugar; beat till fluffy. Add eggs and beat well.

1 16-ounce can (1½ cups) chocolate-flavored syrup
1¼ cups all-purpose flour
1 cup chopped walnuts
Quick Chocolate Glaze

● Stir in the chocolate-flavored syrup. Add the all-purpose flour; mix well. Stir in the chopped walnuts. Spread into the prepared pan. Bake in a 350° oven for 30 to 35 minutes or till done. Cool for 10 minutes on wire rack. While warm, pour Quick Chocolate Glaze atop. Cool completely. Cut into bars. Makes 32 bars.

● **Quick Chocolate Glaze:** In a small saucepan stir together ⅔ cup *sugar,* 3 tablespoons *milk,* and 3 tablespoons *butter or margarine.* Cook and stir over medium heat till the mixture is boiling. Boil for 30 seconds. Remove from heat. Stir in ½ cup *semisweet chocolate pieces* till melted.

Vanilla Cream Pie

TIME:
20 minutes preparation
12 minutes cooking

EQUIPMENT:

medium saucepan	small bowl
dry measures	fork
wooden spoon	measuring spoons
liquid measure	rubber spatula

---

1 cup sugar **½ cup all-purpose flour** **Dash salt** **3 cups milk**	● In a saucepan stir together sugar, flour, and salt. Gradually stir in milk. Cook and stir over medium heat till thickened and bubbly. Cook and stir 1 minute more. Remove from heat.

---

4 beaten egg yolks	● In a small bowl gradually stir about *1 cup* of the hot mixture into the egg yolks. Return all to saucepan. Bring to a gentle boil. Cook and stir 2 minutes more. Remove from heat.

---

3 tablespoons butter *or* margarine, cut up **1½ teaspoons vanilla**	● Stir the butter or margarine and the vanilla into the hot milk mixture.

---

1 9-inch Baked Pastry Shell (see recipe, page 84) **Meringue (optional—see recipe, page 85)**	● Spread the hot mixture into the Baked Pastry Shell. If desired, immediately prepare Meringue. Spread Meringue over hot mixture; seal to edge. Bake in a 350° oven for 12 to 15 minutes or till golden. Cool. Cover; store in the refrigerator. Makes 8 dessert servings.

Banana Pie: **Prepare Vanilla Cream Pie as directed, *except* slice 3 bananas into the shell before turning filling into it. Omit Meringue; slice 1 *banana* atop. Drizzle with *chocolate-flavored syrup.***

Piña Colada Pie: Prepare Vanilla Cream Pie as directed, *except* decrease milk by ¼ cup. Stir ¼ cup *rum*, one drained 8¼-ounce can *crushed pineapple*, and 1 cup *coconut* into the mixture along with vanilla.

Dark Chocolate Pie: Prepare Vanilla Cream Pie as directed, *except* increase sugar to 1¼ cups. Chop 3 squares (3 ounces) *unsweetened chocolate* and add with milk to filling. Omit Meringue; dollop with *whipped cream* and sprinkle with grated *chocolate*.

Baked Pastry Shell

TIME:	EQUIPMENT:	
15 minutes preparation	medium bowl	fork
10 minutes cooking	dry measures	rolling pin
	measuring spoons	9-inch pie plate
	wooden spoon	kitchen shears
	pastry blender	wire rack

1¼ cups all-purpose flour	● In a medium bowl stir together the all-purpose flour and the salt.
½ teaspoon salt	

1 Use a pastry blender in an up-and-down motion or two knives in a crisscross motion to cut the shortening into the flour till the pieces are the size of small peas. Be careful not to completely blend the flour with the fat.

⅓ cup shortening *or* lard	● Using a pastry blender or two knives, cut the shortening or lard into the flour mixture till pieces are the size of small peas. Sprinkle *1 tablespoon* of the water over part of the mixture; gently toss with a fork. Push to side of bowl. Repeat till all of the mixture is moistened. Use your hands to form dough into a ball.
3 to 4 tablespoons cold water	

● On a lightly floured surface, flatten dough with hands. Use a rolling pin to roll dough from center to edges, forming a circle about 12 inches in diameter. Wrap pastry around rolling pin. Unroll into a 9-inch pie plate. Ease pastry into pie plate. *Do not* stretch pastry.

Use kitchen shears to trim pastry to ½ inch beyond edge of pie plate. Fold edge of pastry under so that it is even with the edge of pie plate. Make a fluted edge. Use a fork to prick the bottom and sides of the pastry. Bake in a 450° oven for 10 to 12 minutes or till golden brown. Cool completely on a wire rack.

2 Add the water 1 tablespoon at a time. Toss with a fork. Repeat till all of the pastry is moistened.

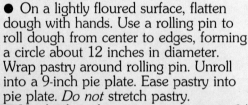

3 Use a rolling pin to roll the pastry from the center to the edges with light, even strokes. Reshape into a circle with your hands as you work.

4 When the pastry is to be baked first without a filling, as for cream pies, prick the bottom and sides of the pastry with a fork. This allows air and steam to escape, which helps prevent the crust from puffing up.

Meringue

TIME: 15 minutes preparation	EQUIPMENT: mixer bowl rubber spatula measuring spoons spoon electric mixer	If you like, you can sprinkle the top of the meringue with coconut before you bake the pie. As the pie bakes, the coconut will become toasty brown.
4 **egg whites** ½ **teaspoon vanilla** ¼ **teaspoon cream of tartar**	● In a small mixer bowl combine the egg whites, vanilla, and cream of tartar. Beat on medium speed of an electric mixer about 1 minute or till soft peaks form (tips curl over).	
½ **cup sugar**	● Gradually add the sugar, about 1 tablespoon at a time, beating on high speed of an electric mixer about 4 minutes more or till mixture forms stiff glossy peaks (tips stand straight) and sugar is dissolved. Immediately drop by spoonfuls atop the hot pie filling, spreading as necessary to cover the filling, and sealing the meringue to the pastry. Use back of spoon to make swirls and peaks in the meringue. Bake according to the pie recipe.	

Beating Egg Whites

Beating the egg whites the right amount of time before and after adding the sugar is very important in making meringues. Before you start adding sugar, beat the egg whites just till soft peaks form (that's when the tips of the egg whites curl over—see page 88). If you beat the egg whites too much before the sugar is added, they won't fluff as high and will look curdled. Once you've added the sugar, beat the egg whites just till glossy stiff peaks form (that's when the tips stand straight—see page 88). If you beat the egg whites too much, the meringue will be dull; if you beat the egg whites too little, the meringue will shrink excessively.

1 Hold the chilled, cracked egg over a custard cup. Slip the yolk from one shell half to the other, allowing the egg white to fall into the cup.

2 Beat the egg whites on high speed of an electric mixer till soft peaks form (tips curl over).

3 Gradually add the sugar as you continue to beat the egg whites till stiff peaks form (see tip, page 87). The egg whites should look white, moist, and glossy. When you pull up the beaters, the peaks will stand straight.

Vanilla Dessert Soufflé

TIME: 45 minutes preparation 55 minutes cooking	EQUIPMENT: aluminum foil 1½-quart soufflé dish small saucepan measuring spoons dry measures wooden spoon	liquid measure small mixer bowl electric mixer rubber spatula large mixer bowl table knife	Soufflé comes from the French word meaning puffed up—and puffed up is the perfect way to describe a soufflé! The light, airy texture of a soufflé comes from beating the egg whites to stiff peaks. What you are actually doing is beating air into the egg whites. Then, when the souffle is cooked, the air expands, causing the soufflé to rise and become puffy.
Butter *or* **margarine** **Sugar**	● Attach a buttered and sugared collar to a 1½-quart soufflé dish. For collar, measure enough foil to go around dish plus a 2- to 3-inch overlap. Fold foil into thirds lengthwise. Lightly butter one side. Sprinkle with sugar. With buttered side in, position foil around outside of dish, letting collar extend 2 inches above top of dish; fasten with tape. Set aside.		
3 tablespoons butter *or* **margarine** **¼ cup all-purpose flour** **⅔ cup milk**	● In a small saucepan melt the 3 tablespoons butter or margarine. Stir in the flour. Add the milk all at once. Cook and stir over medium heat till mixture is very thick and just begins to bubble. Remove from heat.		
4 egg yolks **2 teaspoons vanilla**	● In a small mixer bowl beat the egg yolks on high speed of an electric mixer till the egg yolks are thick and lemon colored (about 5 minutes). Beat in vanilla. By hand, gradually stir the thickened milk mixture into the egg yolk mixture. Wash beaters thoroughly.		
4 egg whites **¼ cup sugar**	● In a large mixer bowl beat the egg whites till soft peaks form (tips curl over). Gradually add sugar, beating till stiff peaks form (tips stand straight). Fold the yolk mixture into the whites, using a down-up-and-over motion. Turn into the prepared soufflé dish.	When the minimum baking time is up, carefully open the oven door and test the soufflé for doneness by gently inserting a knife just off center. If the knife comes out clean, the soufflé is done. If it does not, continue to bake the soufflé.	
	● Bake in a 325° oven about 55 to 60 minutes or till a knife inserted near center comes out clean. Remove foil collar. Serve immediately. Makes 6 dessert servings.		

Chocolate Soufflé

• Prepare the Vanilla Dessert Soufflé (see recipe, page 89) as directed, *except* stir 2 melted and cooled squares (2 ounces) unsweetened *chocolate* into the egg yolk mixture. Continue as directed in the recipe.

Grand Marnier Soufflé

• Prepare the Vanilla Dessert Soufflé (see recipe, page 89) as directed, *except* omit ¼ cup of the milk. Stir ¼ cup *Grand Marnier* and 1 teaspoon finely shredded *orange peel* into the beaten egg yolk mixture. Continue as directed in the recipe.

Mocha Soufflé

• Prepare the Vanilla Dessert Soufflé (see recipe, page 89) as directed, *except* stir 1 tablespoon instant *coffee crystals* into the melted butter or margarine. Stir 2 melted and cooled squares (2 ounces) unsweetened *chocolate* into the egg yolk mixture. Continue as directed in the recipe.

Lemon Soufflé

• Prepare the Vanilla Dessert Soufflé (see recipe, page 89) as directed, *except* stir 2 teaspoons finely shredded *lemon peel* into the egg yolk mixture. Continue as directed in the recipe.

Folding the egg yolk mixture into the egg white mixture is a very important step in making a soufflé. You must be gentle and use the proper folding action (not stirring) or the air that was beaten into the egg whites will be squeezed out. Start by gradually pouring the yolk mixture over the beaten whites. Use a rubber spatula to cut down through the mixture. Scrape across the bottom of the bowl, then bring the spatula up and over the mixture, close to the surface. Repeat this circular down-up-and-over motion, turning the bowl as you work. Do this as quickly and carefully as possible to keep the batter fluffy.

Frozen Peach Daiquiris

TIME: 10 minutes preparation	EQUIPMENT: blender dry measures liquid measure rubber spatula	Because these daiquiries are made with frozen fruits you can make them all year round. But when fresh fruits are easily available, add a touch of summer by making the simple but attractive garnishes in the photo.
1 12-ounce package frozen unsweetened peach slices ¾ cup light rum ½ cup frozen lemonade concentrate ⅓ cup sifted powdered sugar	● In a blender container combine frozen unsweetened peach slices, light rum, frozen lemonade concentrate, and sifted powdered sugar. Cover and blend till the mixture is smooth.	Just trim each drink with a few fresh raspberry, peach, or strawberry leaves. Then add a few berries or a peach slice.
20 to 24 ice cubes	● With the blender running, add ice cubes, one at a time, through hole in lid, to make about 5 cups mixture. Stop machine, scrape down sides with a rubber spatula, if necessary. Makes 4 (10-ounce) beverage servings.	

Frozen Strawberry Daiquiris

● Prepare the Frozen Peach Daiquiris as directed in the recipe, *except* substitute one 10-ounce package frozen sliced *strawberries* for the frozen unsweetened peach slices and omit the powdered sugar.

Frozen Raspberry Daiquiris

● Prepare the Frozen Peach Daiquiris as directed in the recipe, *except* substitute one 10-ounce package frozen red raspberries for the frozen unsweetened peach slices.

Glazed Appetizer Meatballs

TIME:	EQUIPMENT:	
45 minutes advance preparation	bowl	large saucepan
15 minutes final preparation	fork	wooden spoon
	liquid measure	knife
	dry measures	slotted spoon
	measuring spoons	wooden picks
	shallow baking pan	

You can shape meatballs several different ways. Use the method in Glazed Appetizer Meatballs or try one of these two alternatives: Pat the meat mixture into a ¾-inch-thick rectangle on waxed paper. Cut the rectangle of meat into ¾-inch cubes, and roll each cube into a ball. Or, gently shape the mixture into a log with a ¾-inch diameter. Slice the log into ¾-inch lengths, and roll each piece into a ball.

1 slightly beaten egg ¼ cup milk ⅓ cup cornbread stuffing mix ½ teaspoon dry mustard ⅛ teaspoon pepper	● In a bowl stir together the egg and milk. Stir in the cornbread stuffing mix, dry mustard, and pepper.
1 pound ground beef *or* ground pork	● Add the ground beef or ground pork. Use your hands to thoroughly mix the meat into the cornbread stuffing mixture. Shape the meat mixture into ¾-inch meatballs (use a rounded teaspoon of meat mixture for each). Place meatballs in a large shallow baking pan. Cover and refrigerate till 30 minutes before serving time. Uncover and bake in a 450° oven for 15 to 20 minutes or till done.
⅔ cup water ⅓ cup catsup 2 tablespoons brown sugar	● Meanwhile, in a large saucepan stir together the water, catsup, and brown sugar. Bring the mixture to boiling, stirring frequently.
3 apples, cored, *or* one 15½-ounce can pineapple chunks, drained	● If using apples, cut each apple into eighths, and halve each eighth crosswise. Stir the apple or pineapple chunks into the catsup mixture. Reduce heat. Simmer, covered, for 5 minutes.
1 tablespoon soy sauce 1 teaspoon cornstarch ½ teaspoon ground cinnamon ¼ teaspoon dry mustard	● Stir together the soy sauce, cornstarch, cinnamon, and dry mustard. Stir into the catsup mixture. Cook and stir over medium heat till thickened and bubbly. Cook and stir 2 minutes more.
	● Using a slotted spoon, transfer the cooked meatballs into the catsup mixture; heat through. Keep meatball mixture warm. Serve with wooden picks or cocktail picks. Makes about 48.

Index